Agricultural Education
The Occupational Aspirations

Agricultural Education
The Occupational Aspirations

Mohammad Rahim

M S Nataraju

AUTHORSPRESS

Publishers of Scholarly Books

Worldwide Circulation through Authorspress Global Network
First Published 2011
by
Authorspress
E-35/103, Jawahar Park
Laxmi Nagar, Delhi-110 092
e-mail: authorspress@yahoo.com

Agricultural Education: The Occupational Aspirations
ISBN 978-81-7273-575-3

Printed in India at Tarun Offset, Delhi.

Preface

Agriculture and allied fields in India provide ample scope to rural youth for self-employment. Consequent upon the process of liberalisation, privatisation and globalisation many farm based industries are established in the area for agro-processing, seeds, fertilizers and pesticides. Thus, employment opportunities are wide open to agriculture graduates. Hence, agriculture education and training are to be tuned to fit the students to the job requirement of our growing economy.

Education and training are an integral part of development required to update the knowledge, understanding, skill and coping to changes happening in and around the organisation and environment to carry forward the concerned assigned activities by the personnel in any organisation. They help in building capacities among the employees to attain their responsibilities with regained vigour, new technologies, new knowledge and skill through which they get satisfaction and organisation to which they belong are also benefited. This helps a person in cultivating appropriate and desired behavior and attitude towards work and people. Hence, curriculum development, taken up systematically, can make the educational process better and help in building the human resource when there are options to choose the jobs by the students in various institutions develop varying degrees of aspirations towards different jobs.

In this context, the findings of the study conducted at the University of Agricultural Sciences, Bangalore, are discussed in the book, and relevant implications are drawn. The book will be of value to agricultural educators, extension workers and scientists belonging to public, private, NGO and other development sectors as it provides new insights into the occupational aspirations of farm graduates. Above all, the book will be useful to the planners, policy makers and administrators to develop appropriate strategies to fulfil the aspirations of these future generations of India.

Mohammed Rahim
M.S. Nataraju

Contents

1

Aspiration and Its Importance in Agricultural Education

The primary aim of establishing agricultural colleges is to train and educate the students, so that they could engage in agriculture, carryout various activities in scientific manner and thereby boost the production. Similarly, these graduates are expected to be well equipped with knowledge scale required for employment in agriculture, public and private sector. In this modern age, it is imperative to know the choice of career of agricultural students and to prepare them for a satisfied living in their life, as agricultural education offers many job opportunities to plan and choose their career, to reduce dissatisfaction in their job.

The term aspiration refers to a person's orientation toward a goal. Occupational aspiration is a person's desire for an ultimate occupational status attainment. Further, knowledge of aspiration of the people is important, as a man has notions of desirability regarding his future status and does believe that by his own selection and decision he can materially affect the role he will acquire and discharge (Kuvlesky and Bealer, 1967).

The educational system acts as a mechanism for training youth and to perform well in a complex, interdependent and highly organised occupational system. Important changes are on in the occupational structure and in its relationship to the educational system, i.e., many job oriented and occupational related educational systems are coming up, for example, management, vocational and self-employment courses. It becomes necessary for us to know the aspirations of the rural youth on these new occupations. The basic task of preparing youth to perform well in complex occupations rests on the schools and colleges. Youth population in India, in the age group of 14-35 years, is nearly half of the total population. Of this, 20 per cent are urban while the remaining 80 per cent are rural youth. Only around 10 per cent of the youths are skilled in rural areas compared to 22 per cent in urban areas in India. Migration tends to be common among the youth. An inquiry into the occupational aspirations of youth has therefore, special relevance in a developing country like India. The economic changes initiated during the post-independence era have set in motion certain processes that have a substantial impact on aspirations of youth in particular, and new industries, new jobs and new techniques inevitably affect traditional roles and relationships, paving way for new creations. Since all the major roles of the future society are to be shouldered by the present day youth, a study of their occupational aspirations will provide an important clue.

Need for the Study

One of the potential fields, which can provide self-employment opportunities for rural youth in India, is agriculture and allied fields. The prominence of agriculture in the economy of the nation and ever increasing requirements for our teeming millions further widens its scope. It is understood that the capabilities of the youth if properly channelised would bring about immense changes in agriculture and allied fields and it would also minimise the number of unemployed. If proper training in various self employment avenues in agriculture is imparted to the youngsters, it would be developed as a source of income and it would eventually lead to the making of a prosperous society. People believe that education is not very important for those entering farming. But to perform effectively in a highly competitive agricultural market depends on the same sets of high level abilities that are required for competence as in the non-farm occupations. It follows that education is closely tied to effective performance in farming just as it is in other occupations. Doubtless, these ties will become stronger as time goes on.

Youth force is the country's strength, and it is in the country's interest that we need to pay attention to the specific needs and problems of its youth. The problems of youth are, however, compounded and complicated by the socio economic factors in the environment. Extraordinary advances in various disciplinary nevertheless, promise a deeper comprehension of today's youth. One of the major critical choice points which occur in the lives of most men in modern society is the choice of an occupation which not only determines once income and standard of living but influence once social status, sense of identity and worth. Satisfaction in work contributes to personal growth and self fulfillment, dissatisfaction in work may add up to frustration and lack of meaning and purpose in life. A person's level of occupational aspiration is a limited range on the occupations prestige hierarchy which he views desirable or possible for him that consists of his conception of a set of occupations within limited occupational prestige range, which on its lower level is acceptable to him and on its higher level is within the range of feasibility. It is not necessary at all for any one particular person to conceive of these occupations as a part of hierarchy, although most probably do. It is only necessary that objectively the occupations be so located in the social structure. For the local concern of the present research, the basic questions which may be relevantly raised are" Who aspires for what occupation? How? And the present research attempts to answer these questions by unmasking the correlates of occupational aspirations, in terms of social and cultural determinants and exploring the decision making process in the occupation choosing. The present investigation was therefore designed to determine the relationship between socio-economic variables and occupational aspirations of college going youth.

Statement of the Problem

The University of Agricultural Science (UAS), Bangalore, in Karnataka state, was established in 1964 and it was bifurcated into two Agricultural universities in the state, viz., University of Agriculture Sciences, Bangalore, and University of Agricultural Sciences, Dharwad in October 1986. The University of Agricultural Sciences, Bangalore, at present has six teaching campuses and offers undergraduate degree programmes in Agriculture, Agricultural Marketing and Cooperation, Sericulture, Forestry, and Agricultural Engineering. Further, these colleges produce over 300 farm graduates every year. These students have different socio-economic, psychological and cultural backgrounds. Also they differ in their earlier educational setting like, medium of instruction, system of education, peer circle, etc. With such varying backgrounds one cannot expect all the students to have similar aspirations. It is essential to understand the various aspirations and variations in aspirations existing among the students of agricultural colleges because it decides their future career, and hence the study has been attempted with the prime objective to find out the aspiration differences existing among the undergraduate students of different campuses of UAS. A careful assessment of the aspirations of these students will help the administrators and policy makers in fine-tuning the curriculum to suit the requirement of the students. Hence, the present study was contemplated with the following specific objective:

Objectives

1. To study the personal and socio-economic profile of students.
2. To analyse the occupational aspirations of students.
3. To find out the occupational aspiration differences existing among the students of different campuses.
4. To find out the association between socio-economic and personal characteristics with occupational aspirations of students.
5. To study the sources oı information utilised by students for occupation and job opportunities.

Scope of the Study

Students unemployment is increasing day by day and there is substantial student's unemployment in Karnataka state. Therefore, the present study with reference to occupational aspiration and socio-economic status would help to develop a suitable pıogramme and training for students, thereby providing scope for minimising the unemployment. This study, probing the occupational aspirations of students in agriculture university, is a contribution to the field of extension education as well as the university to tailor the curriculum to suit the needs and interests of students so as to reduce the unemployment and underemployment problem.

Limitations of the Study

1. This study is a student's research work and hence there is a limitation of time and resources.
2. Although the University of Agricultural Science, Bangalore, has six teaching campuses in its jurisdiction, only three teaching campuses were purposively chosen for the study.
3. The present study was confined only to B.Sc. (Ag.) students as the major emphasis is on occupational aspiration of students.
4. The study was carried out only with a few variables due to time constraints.

2

Analysis of Occupational Aspirations of Agriculture Students

This study being the pioneer one on occupational aspiration of students at University of Agricultural Sciences, Bangalore, a careful attempt has been made to delineate the methodological procedure for the study. The procedure followed in this study is presented under the following headings:

1. Locale of the Study
2. Selection of Respondents
3. Variables and their measurement
4. Method of data collection
5. Statistical tools used

Locale of the Study

The research study on occupational aspirations of students at UAS Bangalore was conducted during September-November; 2009. The University of Agriculture Sciences, Bangalore, has six teaching campuses, namely, Agricultural College, GKVK Campus, Bangalore, Agricultural College, Mandya, Agricultural College, Shimoga, Sericultural College, Chintamani (Kolar District) and Forestry College, Ponnampet (Coorg District). B.Sc (Ag.) Degree programme is being offered in three campuses: (1) Agricultural College, GKVK, (2) Agricultural College, Mandya and (3) Agricultural College, Shimoga. These three campuses were selected purposively to conduct the study because of the following reasons: (i) More than 250 B.Sc (Ag.) students were available from all the three campuses under the semester system and (ii) the same curriculum was offered (homogeneity) in all the three campuses. The research design followed in the study was survey research method.

Selection of Respondents

The respondents for this study included the final year B.Sc (Ag.) students of all the three campuses. A list of all the final year B.Sc (Ag.) Students of the three campuses were obtained from the academic unit of the respective campuses. All the students of three campuses who were available at the time of investigation (September-November 2009) were considered as the population for the study. The sample size selected for the study was 40 students from each campus.

Agriculture College, GKVK, Bangalore, had a strength of 160 students, out of which 40 students were selected randomly. Agriculture College, Mandya, and Agriculture College, Shimoga had 54 and 42 students respectively. The complete enumeration method was employed. The data were collected from those who were available at the time of investigation. Totally 120 students were considered as the sample for the study.

Dependent Variable

Occupational Aspiration

According to Bealer and Kuvlesky "Occupational aspiration refers to a person's desire for ultimate status attainment". Occupational aspiration is operationalised in this study as first choice made by the youth out of a set of recognised occupational opportunities by using modified Census classification of occupation given by Kuvlesky and Bealer (1967). Census classification is a "common sense" rating of socio-economic status. Two principles were used in this classification, i.e., Principle of head workers and hand workers. Professionals, manager, white-collar jobs were referred to as head workers. Skilled, unskilled and farmers were called as hand workers (Gordon, 1968). An important advantage of using this classification is most of the Educational Institutions organise their curriculum roughly around the "head" and "hand" principle. The occupational classification scheme in this study was the modification of the classic census scheme. This classification consists of Professional occupation, Glamour occupation,

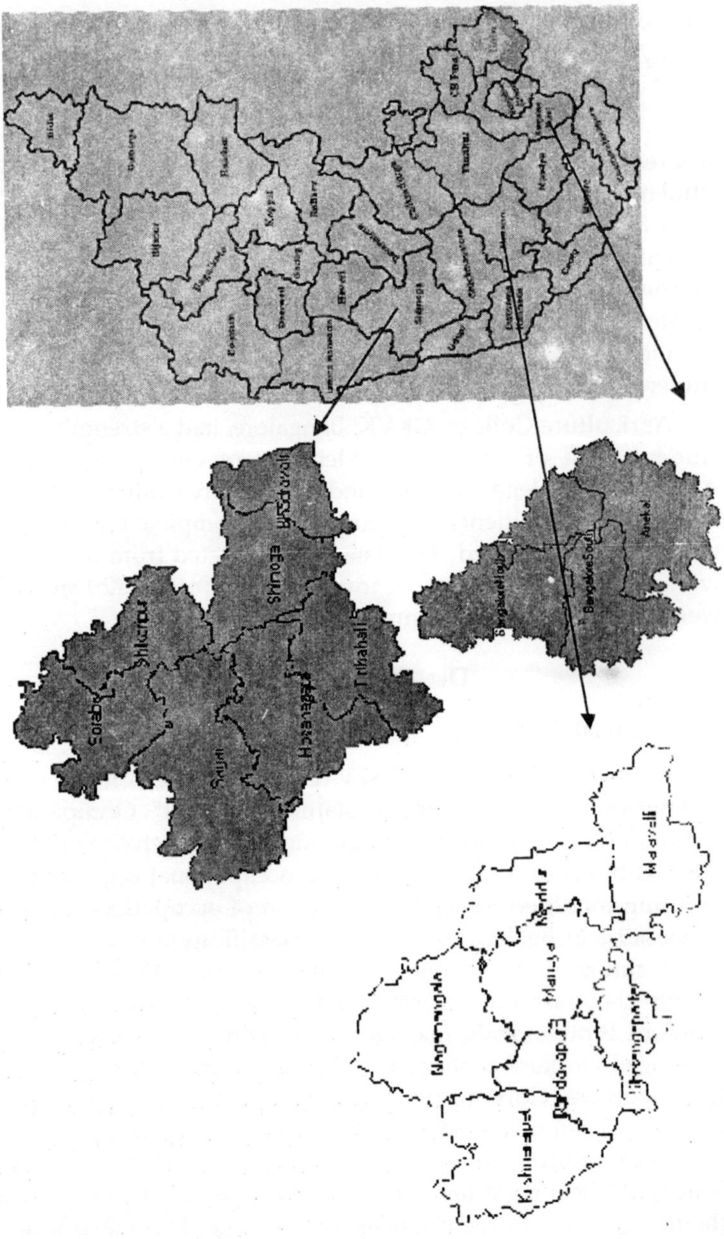

Figure 1. Locale of the Study

Managerial occupation, white collar jobs, skilled jobs, unskilled jobs, Agriculture.

Table 1. Variables and their Measurements

A. Dependent variable	*Measurement*
1. Occupational aspirations	Procedure followed by Sagane (1979)
B. Independent variables	
1. Age	Schedule developed
2. Sex	Schedule developed
3. Birth and native place	Procedure suggested by Hosur (1977)
4. Place of education	Procedure suggested by Hosur (1977)
5. Education level of father	Procedure used by Shivamurthy (1994)
6. Education level of mother	Procedure used by Shivamurthy (1994)
7. Father's occupation	Procedure of Pareek and Trivedi (1964)
8. Mother's occupation	Procedure of Pareek and Trivedi (1964)
9. Parents income	Schedule developed
10.Family type	Procedure of Pareek and Trivedi (1964)
11.Sibling status	Procedure followed by Ashok Kumar (1987)
12.Academic Performance	Procedure followed by Ashok Kumar (1987)

Agricultural occupation classification was done by Hoover (1963). This classification with some modification was used in this study. He has classified agricultural occupation into professional occupation, management occupation, sales and farming occupation. An exhaustive list of 30 occupations were prepared and discussed with experts for their relevancy and finally twenty types of occupations were included in interview schedule. Occupational aspiration was sought in a forthright manner by asking?" "What occupation would you like to follow as the lifetime goal" After completing degree three blanks for answers labelled "first preference", "second preference" and "third preference" were offered to the respondents. Respondents were asked to tick their three choices against the occupations. Scores of 3, 2, and 1 were given for the first, second and third preference, respectively.

INDEPENDENT VARIABLES

Age

Age was operationalised as the number of years completed by the respondents at the time of interview. Respondents of the study were in the age group of 17-25 years. For the purpose of analysis age was classified into three groups:

Age group (years)
Less than 21 years
22-23 years
More than 23 years

Sex

It was operationally defined as whether the respondent is male or female. A score of 2 was given to male respondent and 1 was given to a female respondent.

Birth and Native Place

This variable was operationally defined as the respondent who hails from a rural or an urban background by considering the aspects like birthplace and native place and the scoring procedure suggested by Hosur (1977) is followed in the study.

Items	*Score*
a. Birth place	
i Village	3
ii Taluk	2
iii District	1
b. Native place	
i Village	3
ii Taluk	2
iii District	1

The complete score for this variable was arrived at by scoring up the scores obtained by the respondent on each item. The maximum and minimum scores obtainable by the respondent are 6 and 2.

Place of Education

This is referred to the place of primary, secondary, high school and Pre University education. The procedure suggested by Hosur (1977) is followed in the present study. The scoring procedure is as follows:

Items	Score
a. *Place of completing primary and secondary education.*	
i) Village	3
ii) Taluk	2
iii) District	1
b. *Place of completing high school and pre-university education.*	
i) Village 3	
ii) Taluk	2
iii) District	1

The complete score for the place of education was arrived at by summing up the score obtained by the respondent on each item. The maximum score obtainable by the respondent is 6 and the minimum score is 2.

Education Level of Father

It was operationally defined as the formal education undergone by the respondents father have. The respondents were asked to state the educational level the father and the mother. Quantification of the variable was done using the following procedure suggested by Shivamurthy (1994).

Educational level	*Score*
Illiterate	0
Can read only	1
Can read and write	2
Primary school	3
Middle school	4
High school	5
PUC	6
Graduate and above	7

The maximum and minimum scores obtainable were 7 and 0.

Education Level of Mother

It was operationally defined as the formal education undergone by the respondents mother. The respondents were asked to state the educational level of the mother. Quantification of the variable was done using the following procedure suggested by Shivamurthy (1994). The maximum and minimum scores obtainable were 8 and 0.

Educational level	*Score*
Illiterate	0
Can read only	1
Can read and write	2
Primary school	3
Middle school	4
High school	5
PUC	6
Graduate and above	7

Father's Occupation

This was operationally defined as the occupation performed by the respondents father. The quantification of the variable was done using the following procedure suggested by Pareek and Trivedi (1964):

Occupation	*Score*
Government service	1
Private services	2
Business	3
Labour	4
Farming	5
Caste occupation	6
Any other	7

The maximum and minimum scores obtainable were 7 and 1.

Mother's Occupation

This was operationally defined as the occupation performed by the respondent's mother. The quantification of the variable was done using the following procedure suggested by Pareek and Trivedi (1964):

Occupation	*Score*
Government service	1
Private services	2
Business	3
Labour	4
Farming	5
Caste occupation	6
Any other	7

The maximum and minimum scores obtainable were 7 and 1.

Parents Income

This variable was operationally defined as the annual income obtained by the respondents parents from all the sources. The total annual income obtained by the respondent's father and mother was directly considered for the study.

Family Type

It was operationally defined as total number of persons living in the respondent's family under one roof.

Category	*Score*
Nuclear	1
Joint	2

The score of 1 was given for up to 5 members and 2 were given for above five members.

Sibling Status

It refers to the ordinal position the respondent is born in his/her family. This was categorised into three as the first born, the middle born and the last born. The score 1 was given for the first born, score 2 was given for the middle born, and score 3 was given for the last born.

Category	*Score*
First born	1
Middle born	2
Last born	3

Academic Performance

It was operationally defined as the performance of the students in college for the previous three years. Overall Grade points (OGPA) obtained by the students at the end of the third year was considered for statistical analysis purpose.

METHOD OF DATA COLLECTION

The questionnaire method was chosen to collect the data from the respondents. A well-structured questionnaire was prepared incorporating all the items required for the study. The questionnaire was pre-tested among a group of students who were not the respondents.

Pre-testing was done to avoid ambiguous and clumsy expression. The final questionnaire consisted of the following parts:

PART-A: Profile of students

PART-B: Occupational aspiration

The questionnaire was distributed to the students in their respective campuses after explaining the purpose clearly and collected back.

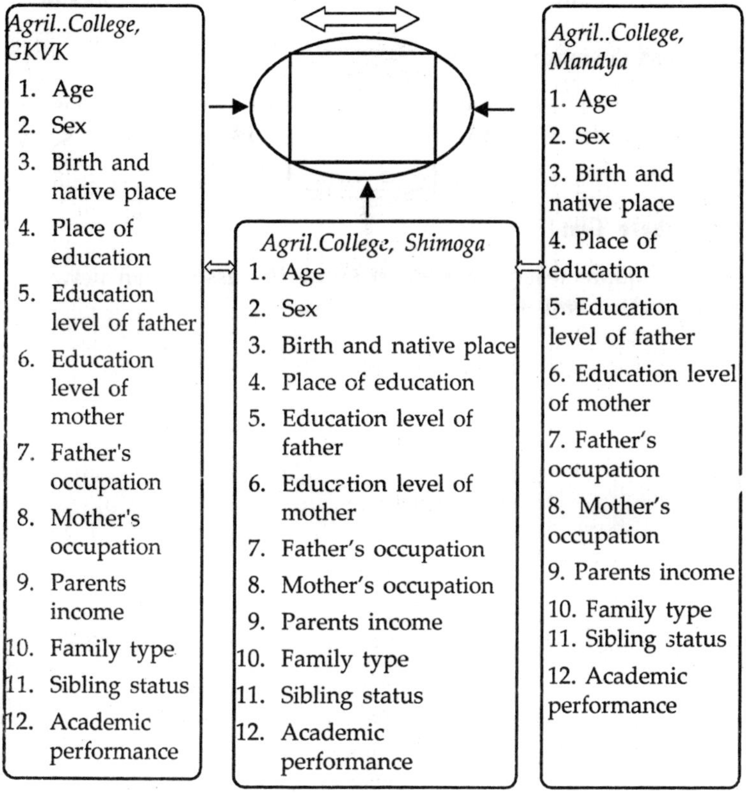

Figure 2. Conceptual Model of the Study

Statistical Tools Used

Frequency

Simple frequency was used to rank the items and make simple comparison.

Percentages

Percentages were used to make simple comparisons of different groups.

Mean

Mean, a measure of central tendency, was used to classify the respondents into different groups based on their score obtained.

Standard deviation

Standard deviation a measure of dispersion was used to classify the respondents into different groups based on their score obtained.

Chi-square Test

The chi-quare test was used to know the association between independent and dependent variables.

3

Socio-economic Aspects of Occupational Aspriations

The findings of the study are discussed and presented under the following headings:

1. Personal and socio-economic profile of students.
2. Occupational aspiration level of students of different campuses.
3. Occupational aspiration differences among the students of different colleges.
4. Association between personal and socio-economic characteristics and aspiration of students.
5. Sources of information utilised for occupation and job placement.

Personal and Socio-economic Profile of Students

The socio-economic profile of students of the Agricultural College at GKVK, Mandya and Shimoga is provided in Tables 1 to10 and the results are presented in the following paragraphs.

Age

The result of Table 1 depicts the distribution of students of different campuses of Agricultural Colleges of UAS, Bangalore, according to their age. It is observed that majority of the students in general belong to less than 21 years age group (57.50 per cent) followed by 22 to 23 years (35.00 per cent) and above 23 years group (7.5 per cent). A similar trend is observed with respect to students of different agricultural colleges wherein more than half of the students belong to below 21 years age group at GKVK (60.00 per cent), Mandya (60.00 per cent) and Shimoga (52.50 per cent) campuses followed by 22-23 years age category 35.0 per cent, 32.5 per cent and 37.5 per cent at GKVK, Mandya and Shimoga Campuses, respectively. The findings seek support from the results reported by Meenaben and Chauhan (2005).

Table 1. Distribution of Students According to Age

(n=120)

Groups	*Agril. College GKVK*		*Agril. College Mandya*		*Agril. College Shimoga*		*Total*	
	No.	*%*	*No.*	*%*	*No.*	*%*	*No.*	*%*
Below 21years	24	60.00	24	60.00	21	52.50	69	57.50
22-23 years	14	35.00	13	32.50	15	37.50	42	35.00
Above 23 years	2	5.00	3	7.50	4	10.00	9	7.50
Total	40	100.00	40	100.00	40	100.00	120	100.00

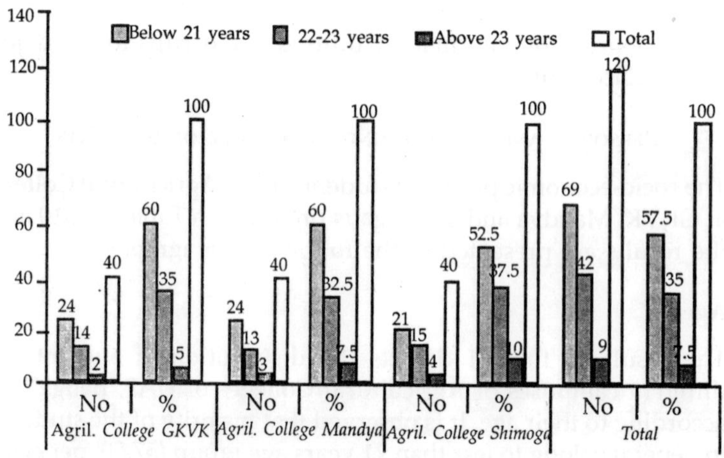

Figure 1. Distribution of students according to age

Sex

A glance at Table 2 shows the distribution of students of different campuses according to sex. A great majority of the students were boys (84.20 per cent) followed by girls (15.80 per cent). Similar findings were true with respect to different colleges. Male domination was observed in GKVK (95.0 per cent), Mandya (82.50 per cent) and Shimoga campuses (75.00 per cent). Less than quarter of the students were girls in the above colleges. The possible reason might be that in the agricultural universities most of the students come from rural background. In rural areas most of the parents give encouragement to the male child and send them for higher studies to urban cities. This finding is in line with that of Rexlin (1993) and Sajeev (2003).

Birthplace and Native Place

As observed in Tables 3 and 4 a large majority of the students in total belong to rural place both with respect to birth (76.70 per cent) as well as native (95.80 per cent) places. Among students of different campuses Shimoga campus had more rural students (85.00 per cent) followed by GKVK (82.50 per cent) and Mandya (62.50 per cent) with respect to birthplace. Similar observations were true with respect to native place with Shimoga 95 per cent, Mandya 95 per cent and GKVK having 97.50 per cent ruralites. Thea agricultural universities are allotted some percentage of reservation for admission to the candidates who are coming from rural areas. Therefore, a majority of them come from rural areas. This finding is strongly supported by that of Makhija and Singh (1987), Abhijit (2002) and Sajeev (2003).

Table 2. Distribution of Students According to Sex

(n=120)

Sex	*Agril. Agril. College GKVK*		*Agril. College Mandya*		*College Shimoga*		*Total*	
	No.	%	No.	%	No.	%	No.	%
Male	38	95.00	33	82.50	30	75.00	101	84.20
Female	2	5.00	7	17.50	10	25.00	19	15.80
Total	40	100.00	40	100.00	40	100.00	120	100.00

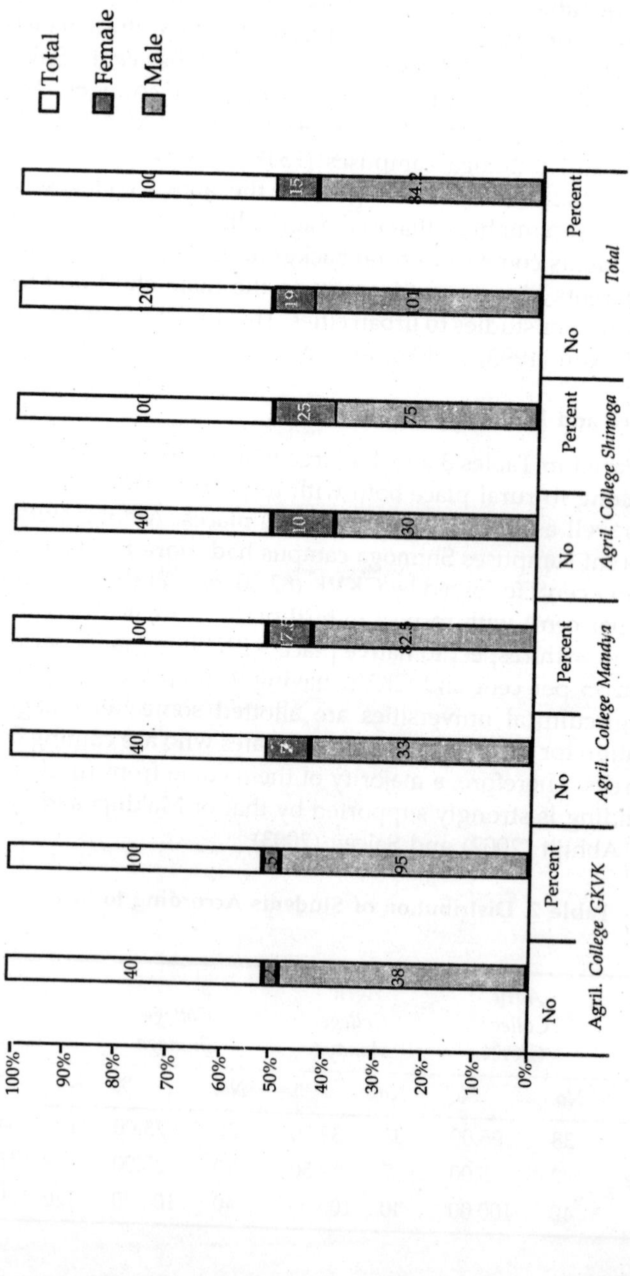

Figure 2. Distribution of Students According to Sex

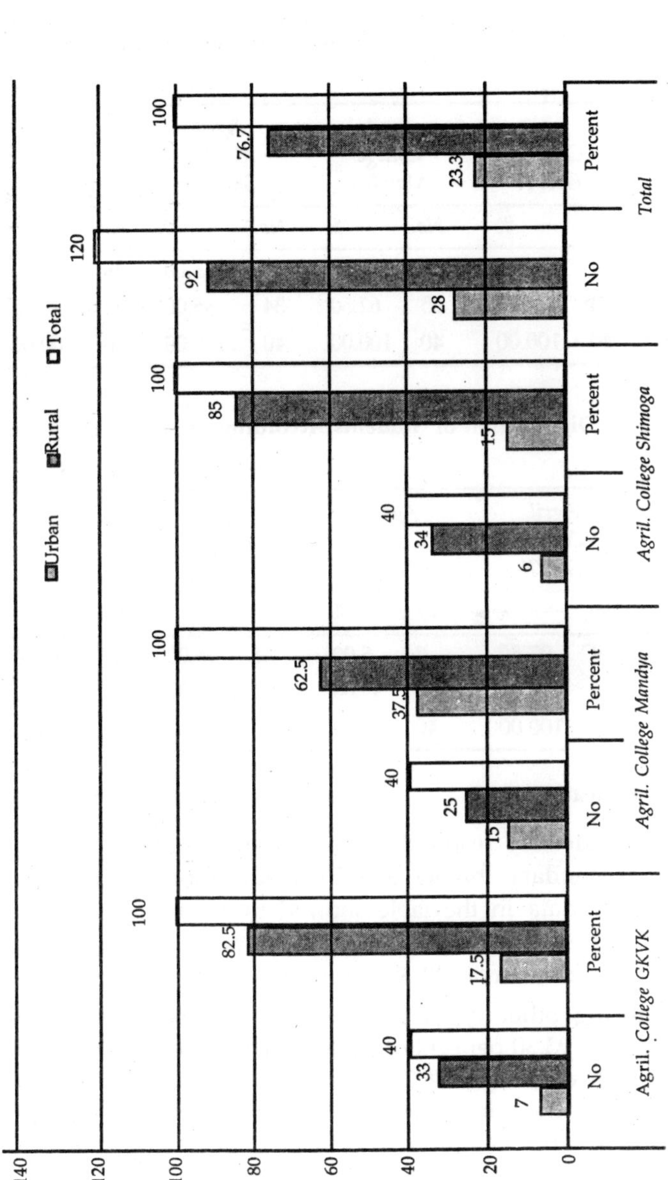

Figure 3. Distribution of Students According to Birthplace

Table 3. Distribution of Students According to Birthplace

(n=120)

Birthplace	*College GKVK*		*Agril. College Mandya*		*Agril. College Shimoga*		*Agril. Total*	
	No.	*%*	*No.*	*%*	*No.*	*%*	*No.*	*%*
Urban	7	17.50	15	37.50	6	15.00	28	23.30
Rural	33	82.50	25	62.50	34	85.00	92	76.70
Total	40	100.00	40	100.00	40	100.00	120	100.00

Table 4. Distribution of Students According to Native Place

(n=120)

Native Place	*Agril. College GKVK*		*Agril. College Mandya*		*Agril. College Shimoga*		*Total*	
	No.	*%*	*No.*	*%*	*No.*	*%*	*No.*	*%*
Rural	39	97.50	2	5.00	38	95.00	115	95.80
Urban	1	2.50	38	95.00	2	5.00	5	4.20
Total	40	100.00	40	100.00	40	100.00	120	100.00

Place of Education

The distribution of respondents according to their places of primary, secondary, higher and PUC education is shown in Table 5. The data in the table showed that a majority of the students had primary education from rural area (70.00 per cent) followed by urban area (30.00 per cent).

Regarding other types of education a reverse trend was observed with 93.30 per cent of students having secondary, 96.70 per cent high school and 96.70 per cent PUC education in urban areas. Exactly the same trend was observed with respect to students of different campuses. As a majority of the student's were born and brought up in rural areas they did their primary education in rural areas. This might be the reason behind this trend. This finding is in conformity with that of Meanaben and Chauhan (2005).

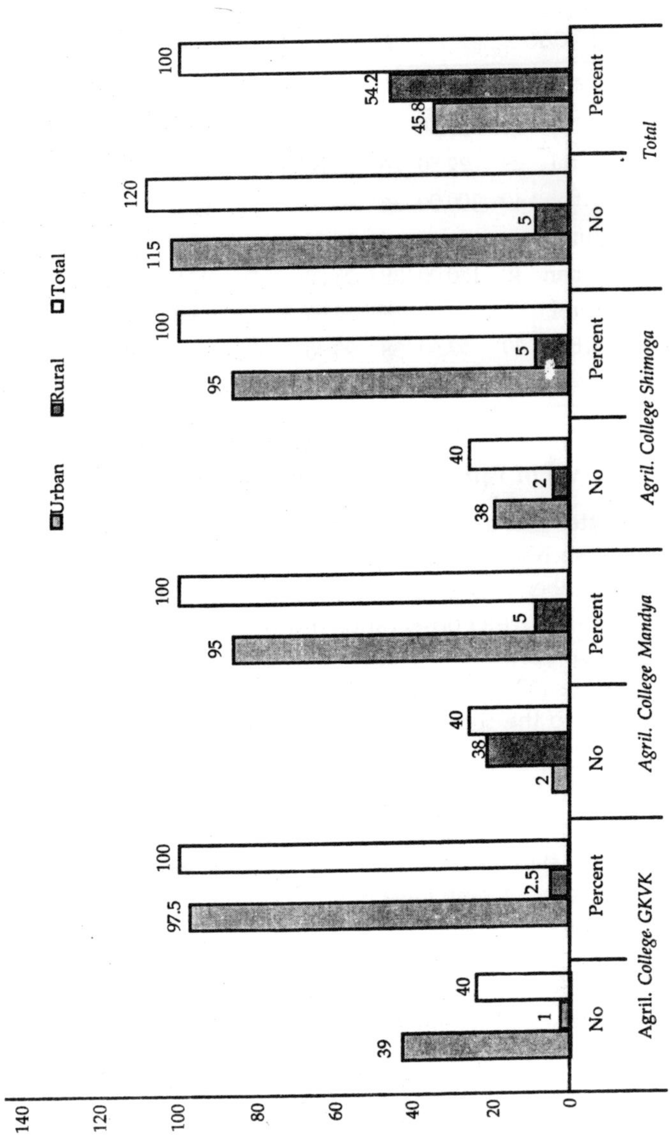

Figure 4. Distribution of Students According to Native Place

Table 5. Distribution of Students According to Place of Education

(n=120)

Education	*Place*	*Agril. College GKVK* No.	%	*Agril. College Mandya* No.	%	*Agril. College Shimoga* No.	%	*Total* No.	%
Primary	Urban	11	27.50	14	35.00	11	27.50	36	30.00
	Rural	29	72.50	26	65.00	29	72.50	84	70.00
Secondary	Urban	40	100.00	36	90.00	36	90.00	112	93.30
	Rural	–	–	4	10.00	4	10.00	8	6.70
High school	Urban	40	100.00	38	95.00	38	95.00	116	96.70
	Rural	–	–	2	5.00	2	5.00	4	3.30
PUC	Urban	39	97.50	38	95.00	39	92.50	116	96.70
	Rural	1	2.50	2	5.00	1	7.50	4	3.30

Educational Level of Father

Table 6 indicates that a majority of the fathers of students (70.00 per cent) had secondary and above level of education followed by an equal number with primary education and illiterates (15.00 per cent each). On further observation it shows that more than half of the fathers of students in Shimoga Campus (80.00 per cent), Mandya Campus (62.50 per cent) and GKVK Campus (67.50 per cent) belonged to the secondary and above education group.

A less number of male parents were illiterates and primary educated. As alluded elsewhere the rural boys were encouraged to get into agricultural universities through agricultural quota, obviously, their parents in rural areas too might have studied more in some cases. A high level of education of the father helps any student to create and have a conducive situation that promotes them towards progress. Further, a high level of education will provide a good understanding regarding various modern ways of advancement for his son/daughter. He motivates them to make the best use of all means of development. This might be the reason behind this trend.

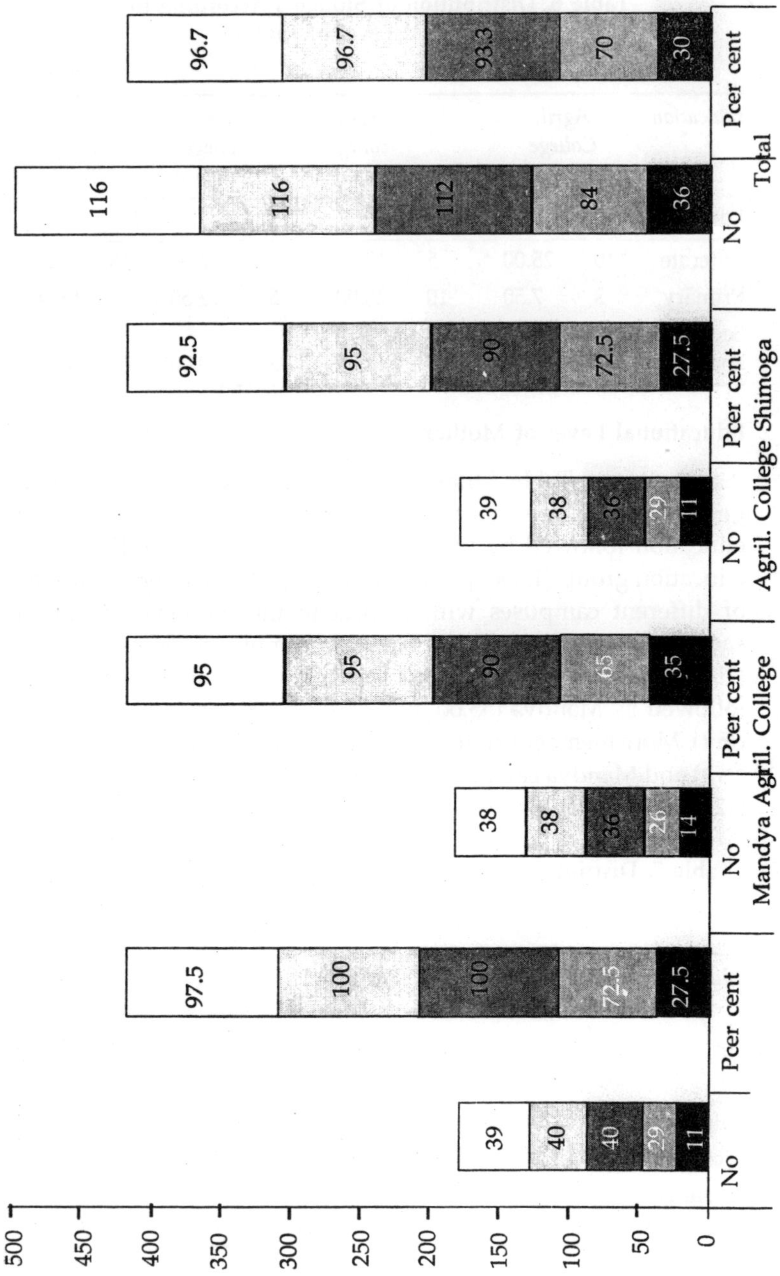

Figure 5. Distribution of Students According to Place of Education

Table 6. Distribution of Students According to Educational Level of Father

(n=120)

Education	*Agril. College GKVK*		*Agril. college Mandya*		*Agril. college Shimoga*		*Total*	
Level	*No.*	*%*	*No.*	*%*	*No.*	*%*	*No.*	*%*
Illiterate	10	25.00	5	12.50	3	7.50	18	15.00
Primary	3	7.50	10	25.00	5	12.50	18	15.00
Secondary and above	27	67.50	25	62.50	32	80.00	84	70.00

Educational Level of Mother

It is seen from Table 7 that a majority of mothers of students in general (60.80 per cent) had secondary and above level of education followed by illiterates (23.30 per cent) and primary education group (15.00 per cent). A comparison among students of different campuses with respect to the mothers education shows that more number of Shimoga campus students mothers (75.00 per cent) belonged to secondary and above education followed by Mandya (55.00 per cent) GKVK campus (52.50 per cent). More members of illiterates were found in GKVK (30.00 per cent) and Mandya campus (17.50 per cent) than Shimoga campus (12.50 per cent).

Table 7. Distribution of Students According to Educational Level of Mother

(n=120)

Education level	*Agril. College GKVK*		*Agril. College Mandya*		*Agril. College Shimoga*		*Total*	
	No.	*%*	*No.*	*%*	*No.*	*%*	*No.*	*%*
Illiterate	12	30.00	7	17.50	5	12.50	28	23.30
Primary	7	17.50	11	27.50	5	12.50	19	15.90
Secondary and above	21	52.50	22	55.00	30	75.00	73	60.80

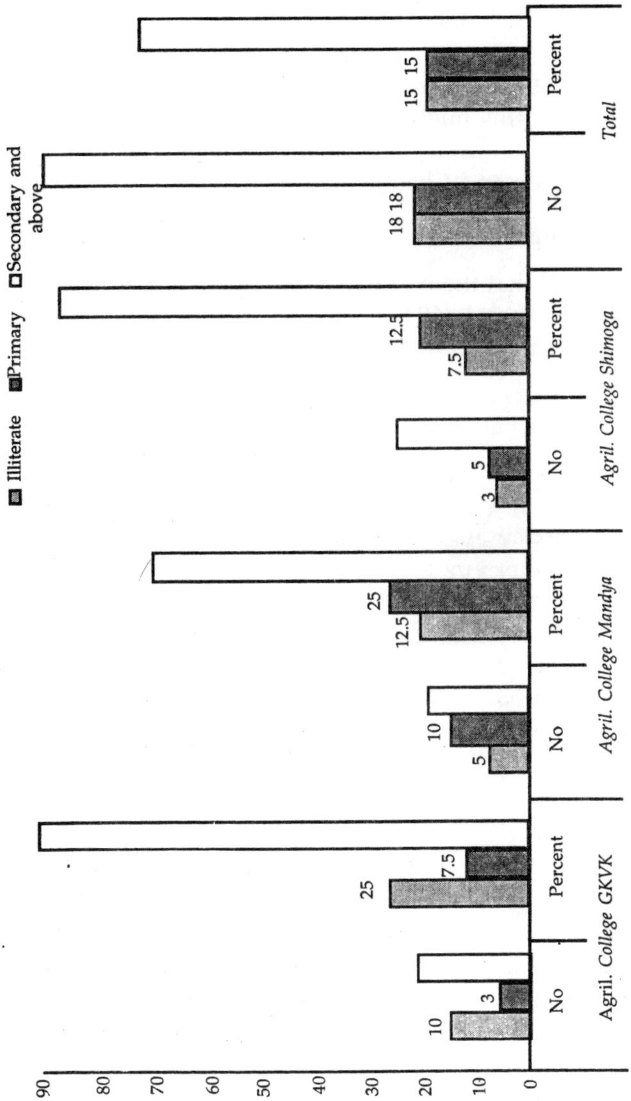

Figure 6. Distribution of Students According to Educational Level of Father

The rural students were encouraged to get into agricultural universities through agricultural quota; obviously, their parents in rural areas too might have studied more in some cases. A mother plays an important role in establishing good habits and tastes of development in her child leading towards an overall development. This might be the reason behind this trend. This finding is in conformity with that of Negga (1987), Bensamuel (1993) Meanben and Chauhan (2005).

Father's Occupation

It is observed that the occupation of fathers of a majority of the students in general (60.8 per cent) had farming followed by business (15.00 per cent) as shown in Table 8.

Table 8. Distribution of Students According Fathers Occupation

(n=120)

Occupation	*Agril. College GKVK*		*Agril. college Mandya*		*Agril. college Shimoga*		*Total*	
Source	*No.*	*%*	*No.*	*%*	*No.*	*%*	*No.*	*%*
1. Government service	3	7.50	4	10.00	1	2.50	8	6.70
2 Private	0	0	1	2.50	2	5.00	3	2.50
3 Business	1	2.50	1	2.50	16	40.00	18	15.00
4 Labour	1	2.50	5	12.50	1	2.50	7	5.50
5 Farming	28	70.00	24	60.00	20	50.00	72	60.80
6 Caste occupation	5	12.50	2	5.00	–	–	–	–
7 Other occupation	2	5.00	3	7.50	–	–	5	4.00
Total	40	100.00	40	100.00	40	100.00	120	100.00

Among different campuses 70 per cent of student's fathers of GKVK College, 60 per cent of students of Mandya College and 50 per cent of fathers of Shimoga college students had farming occupation followed by 40 per cent of fathers of students of

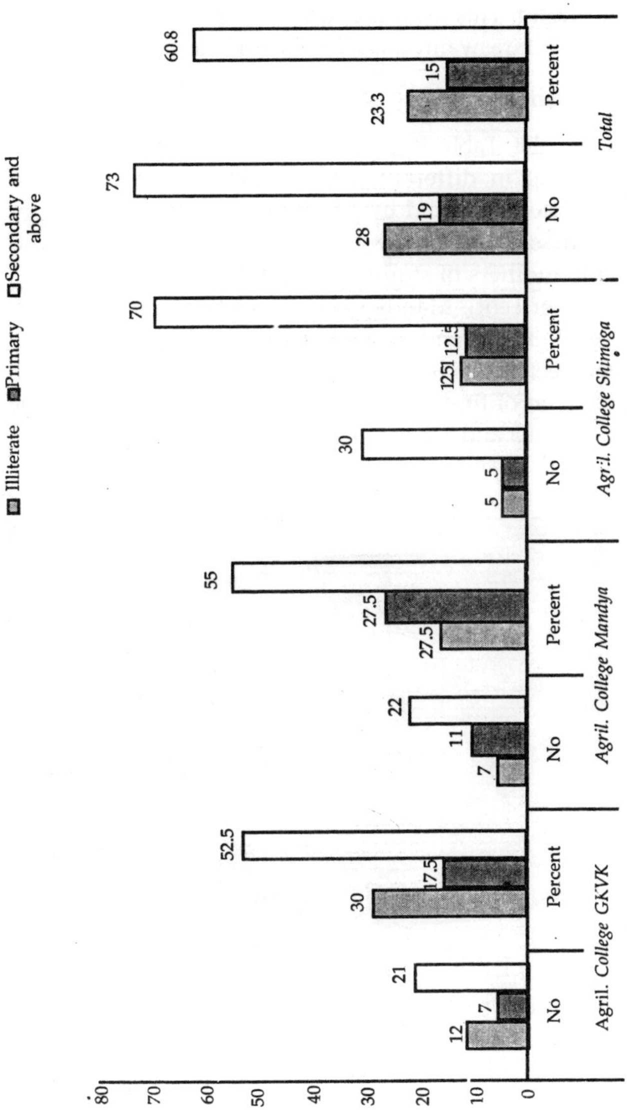

Figure 9. Distribution of students according to education level of their mother

Shimoga college. This trend is obvious, in rural areas, where majority were bent upon farming for their livelihood, which results in this trend. This finding is line with that of Makhija and Singh (1987), Sundaraswami *et al.* (1997) and Waman *et al.* (2000).

Mother's Occupation

It is seen from the Table 9 that a majority of the mothers of students studying in different colleges (57.50 per cent) had farming occupation followed by government service (18.30 per cent) and business (10.90 per cent).A similar trend was observed with respect to mothers of students of different colleges namely, GKVK (75.00 per cent), Mandya (42.50 per cent) and Shimoga (55.00 per cent). This trend is obvious, in rural areas, where a majority were bent up on farming for their livelihood, which results in this kind of finding in this trend. This finding is in line with that of Makhija and Singh (1987), Sundaraswami *et al.* (1997) and Waman *et al.* (2000).

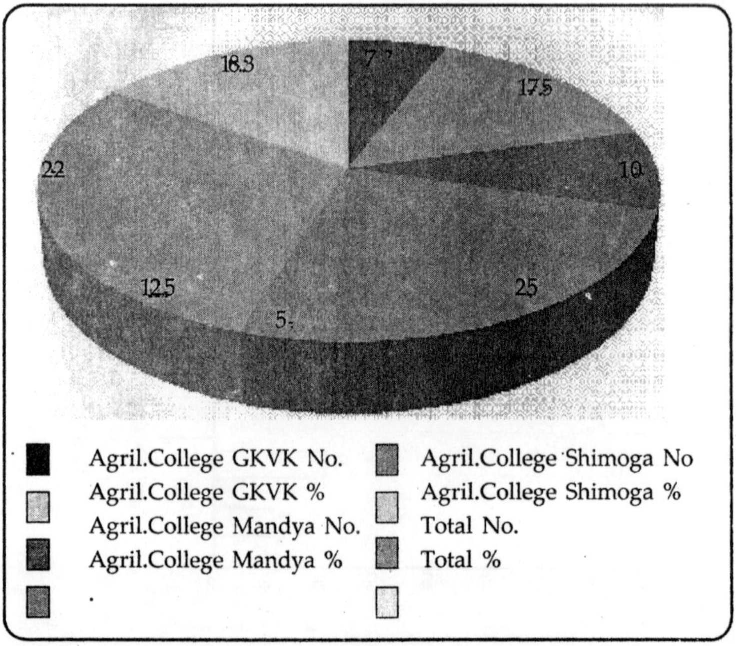

Figure 8. Distribution of Students According to Mother's Occupation

Table 9. Distribution of Students According to Mother's Occupation

(n=120)

Sl. No	*Occupation*	*Agril. College GKVK*		*Agril. College Mandya*		*Agril. College Shimoga*		*Total*	
	Source	*No.*	*%*	*No.*	*%*	*No.*	*%*	*No.*	*%*
1	Government services	7	17.50	10	25.00	5	12.50	22	18.30
2	Private	–	–	3	7.50	1	2.50	4	3.30
3	Business	2	5.00	3	7.50	8	20.00	13	10.90
4	Labour	1	2.50	5	12.50	2	5.00	8	6.70
5	Farming	30	75.00	17	42.50	22	55.00	69	57.50
6	Caste occupation	–	–	2	5.00	2	5.00	4	3.30
	Total	40	100.00	40	100.00	40	100.00	120	100.00

Annual Income

A critical glance at Table 10 reveals the distribution of respondents according to their parents annual income. The results show that in general nearly 60 per cent (59.20 per cent) of the parents had an annual income of Rs.11,000 as against 40.80 per cent income of Rs. 11,000 and above.

Table 10. Distribution of Students According to Annual Income of Parents

(n=120)

Income Level	*Agril. College GKVK*		*Agril. College Mandya*		*Agril. College Shimoga*		*Total*	
	No.	*%*	*No.*	*%*	*No.*	*%*	*No.*	*%*
Less than Rs.11000	27	67.50	21	52.50	23	57.50	71	59.20
Rs.11001 and above	13	32.50	19	47.50	17	42.50	49	40.80
Total	40	100.00	40	100.00	40	100.00	120	100.00

Among different campuses a similar trend was observed with 57.50 per cent of Shimoga, 52.50 per cent of Mandya and 67.50 per cent of GKVK students parents belonging to an annual income category of Rs.11,000 and below. More or less an equal number of respondents of different campuses had an income of Rs.11,000 and above. As the parents were bent upon farming and subsistence type of agriculture, a majority might have belonged to the low income group. This finding is in conformity with that of Rajashekharan (1999) and Waman *et al.* (2000)

Family Type

From a glance at Table 11 it is seen that a large majority of the respondents in total belong to the nuclear family (70.00 per cent) and the remaining belong to the Joint family (30.00 per cent). A similar trend is seen with respect to students of different colleges, namely, GKVK (72.50 per cent), Mandya (65.00 per cent) and Shimoga (72.50 per cent) who belong to the nuclear family. On the other hand 27.5 per cent in GKVK, 35 per cent in Mandya and 27.5 per cent in Shimoga belong to the joint family.

Table 11. Distribution of Students According to Family Type

(n=120)

Type of family	*Agril. College GKVK*		*Agril. College Mandya*		*Agril. College Shimoga*		*Total*	
	No.	*%*	*No.*	*%*	*No.*	*%*	*No.*	*%*
Nuclear	29	72.50	26	65.00	29	72.50	84	70.00
Joint	11	27.50	14	35.00	11	27.50	36	30.00

In the wake of population explosion, the government made a policy of one child per parent and nowadays most of the families in the society prefer the nuclear family. This reason might have influenced this finding. This finding is in agreement with the findings reported by Surywamshi and Wattamwai (2003), and Meenben and Chauhan (2005).

Sibling Status

An overview of data filled in Table 12 delineates the information on sibling status of students of different colleges. Regarding the

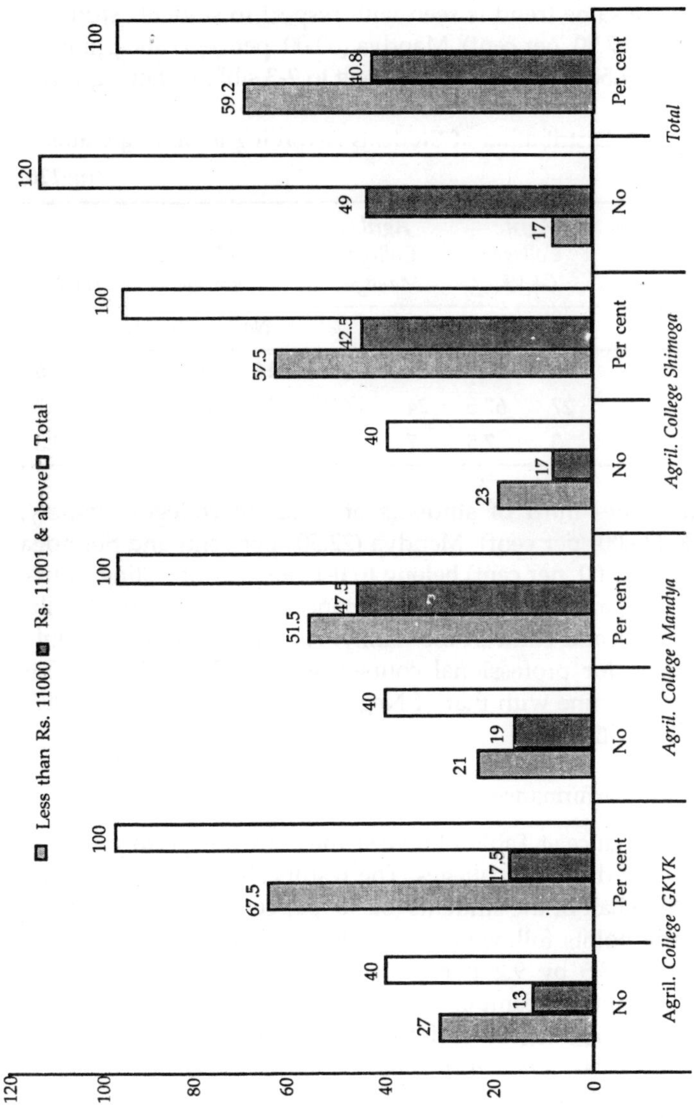

Figue 9. Distribution of Students According to Annual Income of Parents

sibling status of students it is observed that more than half of the respondents belong to group 2-3 (61.70 per cent) followed by 0-1 (27.50 per cent) and more than 3 group (10.80 per cent). More or less the same trend is seen with respect to students studying at GKVK (67.50 per cent), Mandya (60.00 per cent) and Shimoga campus (57.50 per cent) who belong to 2-3 sibling status groups.

Table 12. Distribution of Students According to Sibling Status

(n=120)

Sibling status	*Agril. College GKVK*		*Agril. College Mandya*		*Agril. College Shimoga*		*Total*	
	No.	*%*	*No.*	*%*	*No.*	*%*	*No.*	*%*
0-1	10	25.0	9	22.5	14	35.0	23	27.5
2-3	27	67.5	24	60.0	23	57.5	74	61.7
More than 3	3	7.5	7	17.0	3	7.5	13	10.8

Around one- third of students of different colleges, namely, GKVK (25.00 per cent), Mandya (22.50 per cent) and Shimoga Colleges (35.00 per cent) belong to 0-1 category of sibling status. Obviously parents give more importance or encouragement to the first and second child in the family. As a result majority might have gone for professional courses such as B.Sc. (Agri.). This finding is in line with that of Negga (1987), Sharma *et al.* (1995) and Abhijit (2002).

Academic Performance

A critical glance at Table 13 reveals the academic performance of students of different colleges. The results shows that in general more than half of the students (52.50 per cent) had obtained 7.0-8.5 grade points followed by less than 7.0 by 38.3 per cent and more than 8.5 by 9.2 per cent of students. Among different colleges, Shimoga campus students (67.50 per cent) were more in 7 to 8.5 GPA categories followed by GKVK (37.50 per cent) and Mandya (52.50 per cent). Similar findings were reported by Chauhan *et al.* (1978).

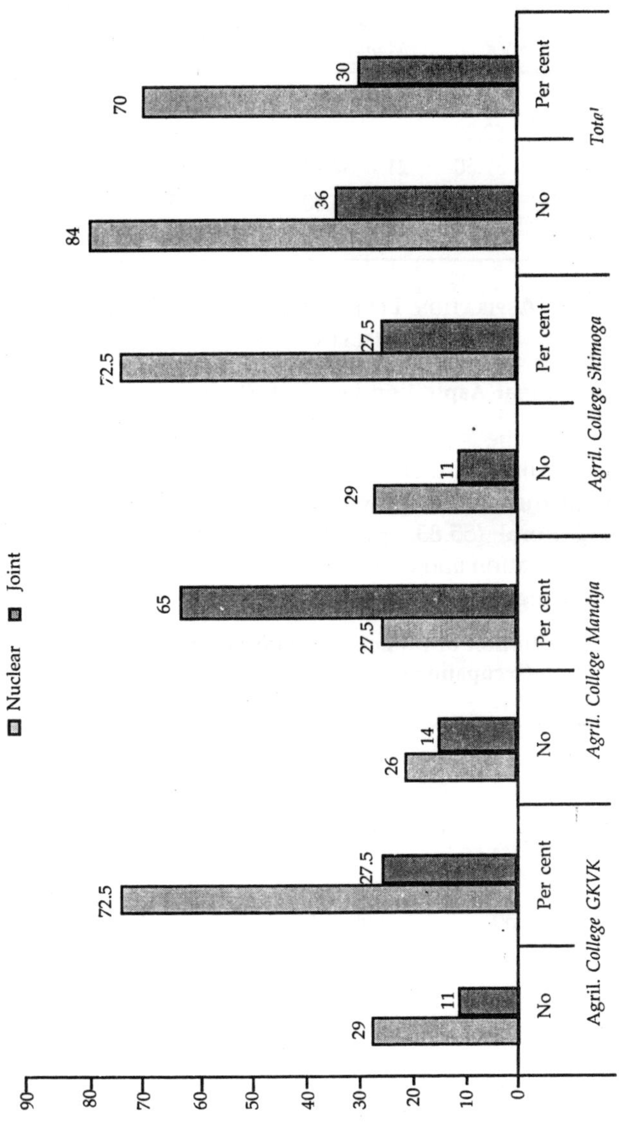

Figure 10. Distribution of Students According to Family Type

Table 13. Distribution of Students According to Academic Performance

(n=120)

Academic Performance	*Agril. College GKVK*		*Agril. College Mandya*		*Agril. College Shimoga*		*Total*	
	No.	*%*	*No.*	*%*	*No.*	*%*	*No.*	*%*
<7.0	25	62.50	9	22.50	12	30.00	46	38.30
7.0-8.5	15	37.50	21	52.50	27	67.50	63	52.50
>8.5	0	0	10	25.00	01	2.50	11	9.20
Total	40	100.00	40	100.00	40	100.00	120	100.00

Occupational Aspiration Level of Students of Different Campuses

Overall Occupational Aspiration Level of Students

Table 14 depicts the students of different colleges of UAS, Bangalore, according to their occupational aspiration level. A cursory look at the results shows that nearly two-thirds of the students in general (55.83 per cent) had a lower level of occupational aspiration and over one-third of the students (34.17 per cent) had a higher level of aspiration.

Table 14. Distribution of Students According to Their Overall Occupational Aspiration Level

(n=120)

Colleges	*Aspiration level*						*Mean*	*SD*
	Low		*Medium*		*High*			
	No.	*%*	*No.*	*%*	*No.*	*%*		
Agril. College GKVK	27	67.50	3	7.50	10	25.00	18.40	19.172
Agril. College Mandya	19	47.50	5	12.50	16	40.00	27.87	11.424
Agril. College Shimoga	21	52.50	4	10.00	15	37.50	25.60	20.262
Overall	67	55.83	12	10.00	41	34.17	23.95	19.877

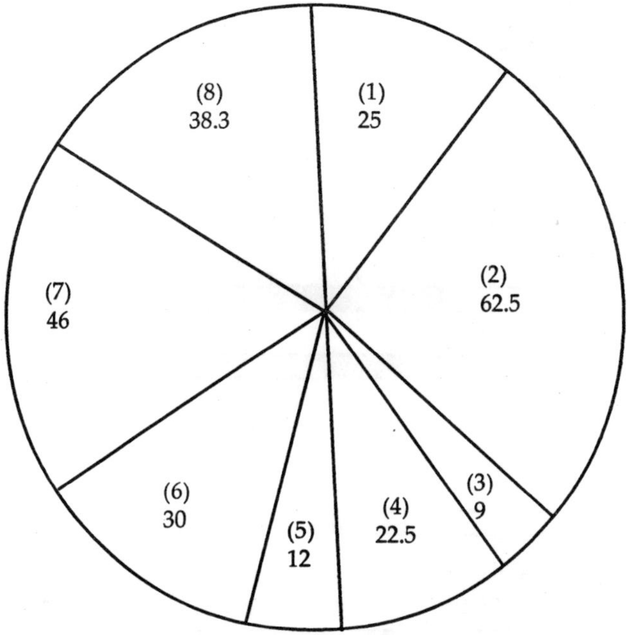

1) Agril.College GKVK No.
2) Agril.College GKVK %
3) Agril.College Mandya No.
4) Agril.College Mandya %
5) Agril.College Shimoga No
6) Agril.College Shimoga %
7) Total No.
8) Total %

Figure 11. Distribution of Students According to Academic Performance

A similar trend of results was true with respect to students of different colleges. More than two- thirds of students of Agricultural College, GKVK, belong to the low aspiration category (67.50 per cent) followed by students of Shimoga (52.50 per cent) and Mandya (47.5 per cent). Regarding the high level of occupational aspiration group more number of Mandya students (40.00 per cent) followed by Shimoga (37.50 per cent) and GKVK students (25.00 per cent) were found.

Difference in Occupational Aspiration Level of Students of Different Campuses

Table 15 shows the difference in occupational aspiration level of students of different agricultural colleges of UAS, Bangalore. The

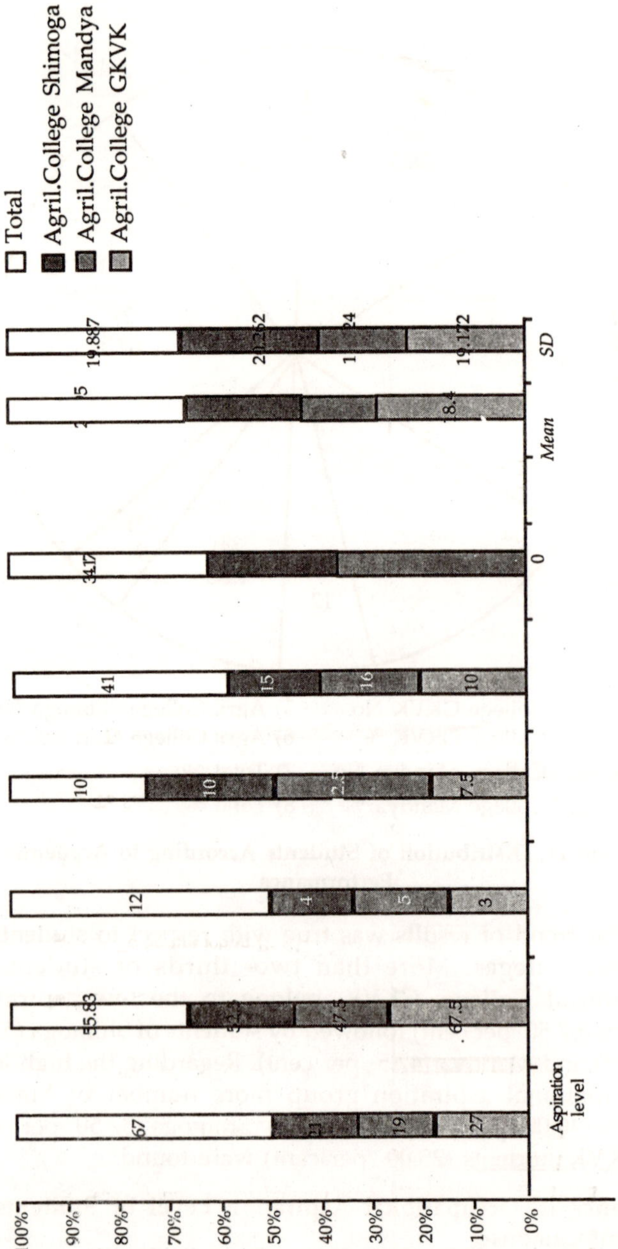

Figure 12. Distribution of Students According to their Overall Occupational Aspiration Level

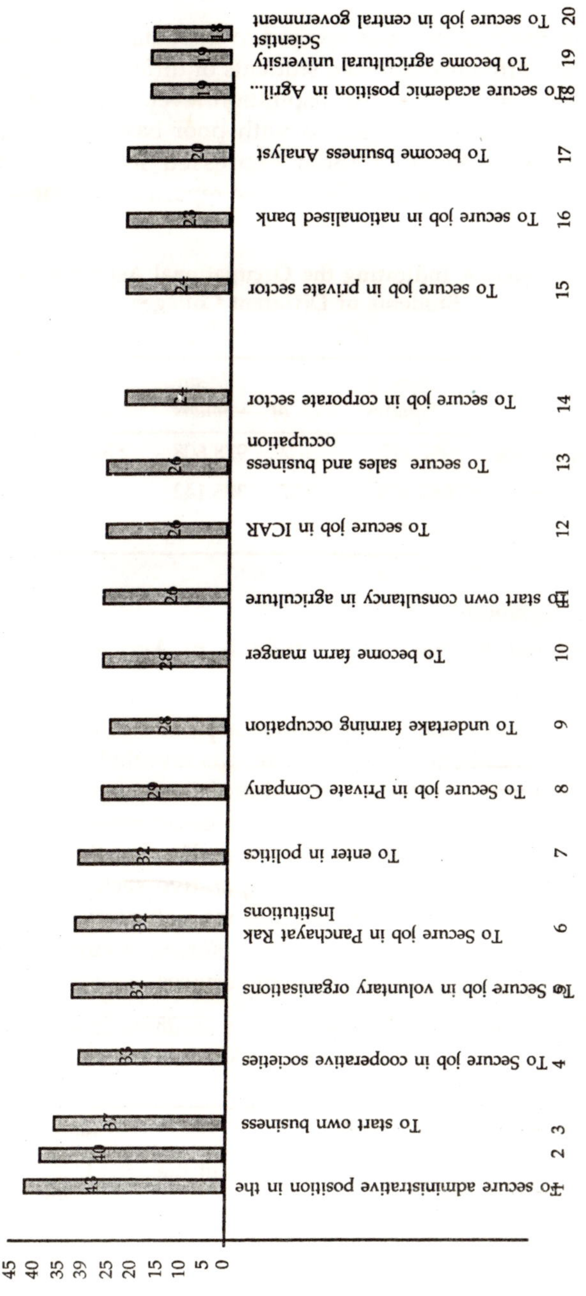

Figure 13. Occupational aspirations of students of Agricultural College, GKVK

results of the ANOVA test applied to the data indicated a non-significant difference between students of different colleges with respect to their occupational aspiration level. A majority of the students had rural background with poor basic amenities and lower income. Most of them expressed low occupational aspiration level. Similar findings were reported by Arunachalam (2000).

Table 15. ANOVA Indicating the Occupational Aspiration Level of Students of Different Colleges

(n=120)

Source of Variation	*Sum of Squares*	*df*	*Mean Square*	*F*	*Sig.*
Between groups	1957.217	2	978.608	2.541	0.083 NS
Within groups	45061.575	117	385.142		
Total	4701.792	119			

Table value 2.99(5 per cent)

NS: Non-Significant

Occupational Aspirations of Students of Agricultural College, GKVK

Table 16 shows the occupational aspirations of students of Agricultural College, GKVK. The results revealed that a majority of the students preferred an administrative position in the department of agriculture and other government departments followed by starting the own business. The fourth rank went in fovour of getting a job in the cooperative sector followed by getting a job in panchayatiraj institutions, voluntary organisations and private companies. The least preferred occupation was to secure a job in central government services.

Table 16. Occupational Aspiration of Students of Agricultural College, GKVK

(n=40)

SI.No.	*Job Aspiration*	*Score*	*Rank*
1	To secure an administrative position in the dept. of agriculture	43	I
2	To secure an Administrative job in government departments	40	II
3	To start one's own business	37	III

4	To secure a job in the cooperative sector	33	IV
5	To secure a job in voluntary organisations	32	V
6	To secure a job in Panchayati raj Institutions	32	V
7	To enter politics	32	V
8	To secure a job in a private company	29	VI
9	To undertake farming occupation	28	VII
10	To become a farm manager	28	VII
11	To start one's own consultancy in agriculture	26	VIII
12	To secure a job in ICAR	26	VIII
13	To secure sales and business occupation	26	VIII
14	To secure a job in the corporate sector	24	IX
15	To secure a job inpPrivate bank	24	IX
16	To secure a job in a nationalised bank	23	X
17	To become a business analyst	20	XI
18	To secure a academic position in Agril. University	19	XII
19	To become an agricultural university scientist	19	XII
20	To secure a job in central government	18	XIII

Occupational Aspirations of Students of Agricultural College, Mandya

A critical look at Table 17 shows the occupational aspirations of students of Agricultural College, Mandya. The results reveal that a majority of the students preferred an administrative position in the department of agriculture followed by getting an administrative job in government departments, an academic position in the agricultural university, getting a job in a private company and the corporate sector. The least preferred occupation was to become a business analyst.

Table 17. Occupational Aspiration of Students of Agricultural College, Mandya.

(n=40)

SI.No.	*Job Aspiration*	*Score*	*Rank*
1	To secure an administrative position in the dept. of agriculture	56	I
2	To secure an administrative job in government departments	54	II
3	To secure an academic position in Agril. University	48	III

4	To secure a job in a private company	48	IV
5	To secure a job in a corporate sector	43	V
6	To secure a job in a panchayati raj institutions	43	V
7	To enter Politics	43	V
8	To secure sales and business occupation	42	VI
9	To undertake farming occupation	42	VI
10	To start one's own business	41	VII
11	To become a farm manager	41	VII
12	To secure a job in a voluntary organisations	41	VII
13	To start one's own consultancy in agriculture	39	VIII
14	To secure a job in ICAR	39	VIII
15	To secure a job in central government	38	IX
16	To secure a job in a nationalised bank	37	X
17	To secure a job in private banks	37	X
18	To become an agricultural university scientist	36	XI
19	To secure a job in the cooperative sector	35	XII
20	To become a business analyst	34	XIII

Occupational Aspirations of Students of Agricultural College, Shimoga

A glance look at Table 18 shows the occupational aspirations of students of Agricultural College, Shimoga. The results show that a majority of the students preferred an academic position in the agriculture university followed by getting an administrative job in government. The fourth rank went in favour of stating one's own business and private company, followed by an administrative position in the department of agriculture, a job in a nationalised bank and business occupation. The least preferred occupation was to secure a job in ICAR.

Table 18. Occupation Aspirations of Students of Agricultural College, Shimoga

(n=40)

SI.No.	*Job Aspiration*	*Score*	*Rank*
1	To secure an academic position in agril. university	56	I
2	To secure an administrative job in government department	54	II
3	To secure a job in a private company	49	III

4	To start one's own business	48	IV
5	To secure an administrative position in the dept. of agriculture	46	V
6	To secure a job in a nationalised bank	44	VI
7	To enter Politics	43	VII
8	To secure sales and business occupation	41	VIII
9	To start one's own consultancy in agriculture	39	IX
10	To secure a job in voluntary organisations	36	X
11	To secure a job in a nationalised bank	33	XII
12	To secure a job in central govt	32	XIII
13	To secure a job in Coperative sector	32	XIII
14	To become a business analyst	32	XIII
15	To become a farm manager	32	XIII
16	To secure a job in panchayati raj institutions	30	XIV
17	To become an agricultural university scientist	30	XIV
18	To undertake farming occupation (dairy, poultry, horticulture, sericulture)	26	XV
19	To secure a job in the corporate sector	25	XVI
20	To secure job in ICAR22		XVII

Occupational Aspirations of Students (Overall)

The results in Table 19 show the occupational aspirations of students of Agricultural College, Mandya, GKVK and Shimoga. The results reveal that the majority of the students preferred an administrative job in government departments followed by securing an academic position in agricultural university. The fourth rank went in favour of starting one's own business and job in a private company followed by an administrative job in the department of agriculture, voluntary organisations and sales and business occupation. The least preferred occupation was to become a business analyst.

In general the results revealed that a majority of the students preferred an administrative job in government departments securing academic position in agricultural university followed by a job in a private company and to start one's own business. The occupations aspired in the next order were to secure job in the agricultural department, voluntary organisations, sales and business occupation, and to become an agricultural university

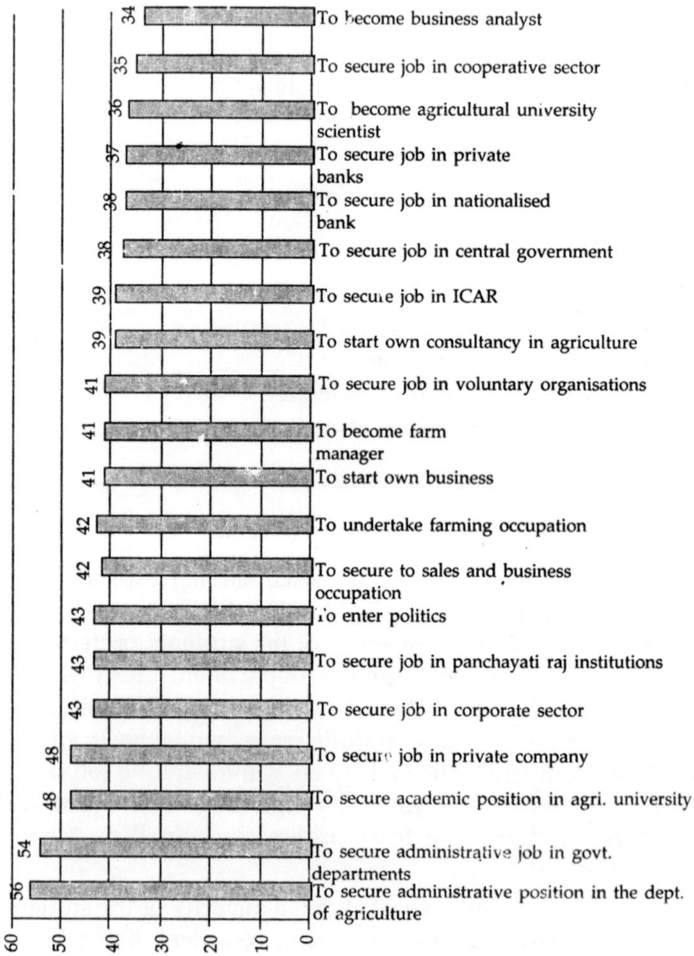

Figure 14. Occupational Aspirations of Students of Agricultural College, Mandya

scientist. This might be because of the security of job in government organisations, high status, pay and perks, and other facilities. Naturally starting of one's own business requires a lot of investment in terms of resources like money, labour, time, materials and also it requires risk bearing ability. This might be the reasons for the above trend of results. The findings are in line with the results reported by Pandey (1974), Arunachalam *et al.* (2000) and Waman *et al.* (2000).

Table 19. Occupation aspirations of students of Agricultural College, (GKVK, Shimoga, and Mandya)

(*n*=120)

SI.No.	*Job Aspiration*	*Score*	*Rank*
1	To secure an administrative job in government departments	140	I
2	To secure an academic position in agril. university	135	II
3	To secure a job in a private company	125	III
4	To start one's own business	123	IV
5	To secure an administrative position in the department of agriculture	118	V
6	To entre politics	110	VI
7	To secure a job in voluntary organisations	109	VII
8	To secure sales and business occupation	108	VIII
9	To become an agricultural university scientist	108	VIII
10	To undertake farming occupation	105	IX
11	To secure a job in panchayati raj institutions	105	IX
12	To secure a job in nationalised bank	104	X
13	To start one's own consultancy in Agriculture	101	XI
14	To become a farm manager	101	XI
15	To secure a job in the Cooperative sector	100	XII
16	To secure a job in cthe corporate sector	100	XII
17	To secure a job in private banks	98	XIII
18	To secure a job in central govt	88	XIV
19	To secure a job in ICAR	87	XV
20	To become a business analyst	86	XVI

Occupational Aspiration Preferences of Students of Agricultural College, GKVK

It is observed from Table 20 that a majority of the students of Agricultural College, GKVK preferred to enter into politics (22.50

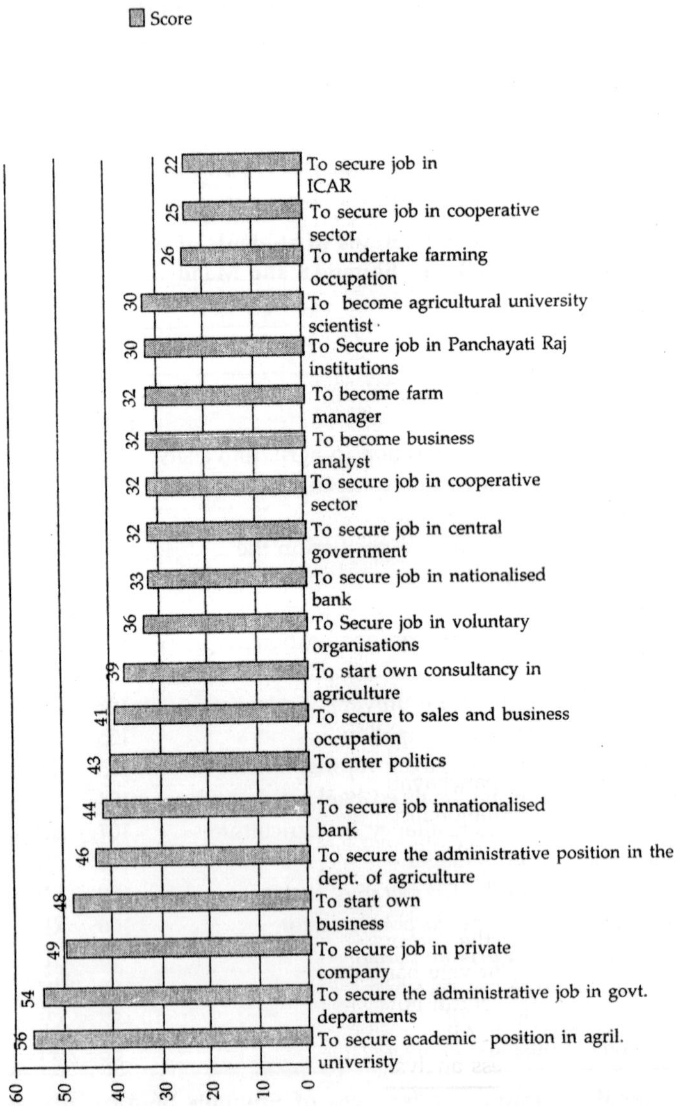

Figure 15. Occupation Aspirations of Students of Agricultural College, Shimoga

per cent) as the third preference followed by securing an administrative position in the Department of Agriculture (17.50 per cent) and to secure a job in voluntary organisations (15.00 per cent) as the least preferred occupations.

Table 20. Occupational Aspiration Preference of Students of Agricultural College, GKVK

(n=40)

Sl. No.	*Job Aspirations*	*III Preference*		*II Preference*		*I Preference*	
		No.	*%*	*No.*	*%*	*No.*	*%*
1	To secure an administrative job	4	10.00	4	10.00	17	42.50
2	To start one's own consultancy in agriculture	3	7.50	4	10.00	9	22.50
3	To secure an academic position in agril. university	1	2.50	4	10.00	8	20.00
4	To become an agricultural university scientist	2	5.00	3	7.50	7	17.50
5	To secure sales and business occupation	4	10.00	6	15.00	2	5.00
6	To start one's own business	4	10.00	8	20.00	12	30.00
7	To become a business analyst	2	5.00	5	12.50	4	10.00
8	To secure a job in central govt	1	2.50	2	5.00	11	27.50
9	To secure a job in the cooperative sector	4	10.00	9	22.50	3	7.50
10	To secure a job in the corporate sector	2	5.00	5	12.50	8	20.00
11	To secure an administrative position in the dept. of agriculture	7	17.50	11	27.50	–	–
12	To undertake farming occupation	3	7.50	8	20.00	3	7.50

13	To become a farm manager	3	7.50	8	20.00	3	7.50
14	To secure job in ICAR	4	10.00	2	5.00	10	25.00
15	To secure job in nationalised bank	1	2.50	7	17.00	6	15.00
16	To secure job in voluntary organisations	6	15.00	4	10.00	6	15.00
17	To secure job in Panchayat Raj Institutions	5	12.50	7	17.50	3	7.50
18	To enter in Politics	9	22.50	2	5.00	1	2.50
19	To secure job in private company	6	15.00	3	7.50	5	12.50
20	To secure job in Private Banks	3	7.50	6	15.00	1	2.50

The second preferred areas are to secure an administrative position in the Department of Agriculture (27.50 per cent) followed to securing job in cooperative societies (22.50 per cent) and undertaking farming occupation. The first choice is in the order of securing an administrative job in the government department (42.50 per cent), securing a central government job (27.50 per cent) and starting one's own consultancy in agriculture (20.00).

Occupation Aspiration Preferences of Students of Agricultural College, Mandya

The Table 21 depicts the occupational aspirations choices among students of Agricultural College, Mandya. The third preferred aspirations were to start a sales and business occupation (20.00 per cent), undertake own farming occupation (20.00 per cent) and to enter politics (20.00 per cent). The second order preferences were to secure an administrative position in the Department of Agriculture (47.50 per cent), followed by securing a job in cooperative societies (27.50 per cent) and panchayathi raj institutions (27.50 per cent). The first preferred areas were in the order of securing an administrative job (57.50 per cent) followed by becoming agricultural university scientist (42.50 per cent) and to secure a job in central government (42.50 per cent).

Table 21. Occupational Aspiration Preferences of Students of Agricultural College, Mandya

(n=40)

Sl. No.	*Job preference*	*III Preference*		*II Preference*		*I Preference*	
		No.	*%*	*No.*	*%*	*No.*	*%*
1	To secure the Administrative job in government departments	5	12.50	8	20.50	23	57.50
2.	To start own consultancy in Agriculture	5	12.50	9	22.50	6	15.50
3.	To secure academic position in Agril. University	7	11.50	8	20.00	11	27.50
4.	To become Agricultural University Scientist	3	7.50	5	12.50	17	42.50
5.	Sales and business occupation	8	20.00	6	15.00	6	15.00
6.	To start own business	7	17.50	8	20.00	4	10.00
7.	To become Business analyst	4	10.00	7	17.50	8	20.00
8.	To secure job in central GOVT	5	12.50	3	7.50	7	42.50
9.	To secure job in Cooperative sector	3	7.50	11	27.50	4	10.00
10.	To secure job in corporate sector	7	45.00	7	17.50	8	20.00
11.	To secure administrative position in the Dept. of Agriculture	2	5.00	19	47.50	12	30.00
12.	To undertake farmingoccupation	8	20.00	8	20.00	2	5.00

13. To become farm Manager	3	7.50	9	22.50	14	35.00
14. To secure job in I C A R	4	10.00	8	20.00	11	27.50
15. To secure job in nationalised bank	3	7.50	9	22.50	10	25.00
16. To secure job in voluntary organisations	7	17.50	6	15.00	8	20.00
17. To secure job in Panchayat Raj Institution	6	15.00	11	27.50	3	7.50
18. To enter in Politics	8	20.00	8	20.00	3	7.50
19. To secure job in Private Banks	5	12.50	8	20.00	6	15.00

Occupational Aspiration Preferences of Students of Agricultural College, Shimoga

The occupational aspirations indicated by the students of Agricultural College, Shimoga is filled in Table 22. The results revealed that a majority of the students preferred to start their own business (30.00 per cent) followed to securing an academic position in the agricultural university (27.55 per cent) as their third preferred occupation.

Table 22. Occupational Aspiration Preferences of Students of Agricultural College, Shimoga

(n=40)

Sl. No.	*Job preference*	*III Preference*		*II Preference*		*I Preference*	
		No.	*%*	*No.*	*%*	*No.*	*%*
1	To secure the administrative job in government department	3	7.50	8	20.00	24	60.00
2	To secure administrative position in the Dept. of Agriculture	1	2.50	13	32.50	17	42.50

3 To secure academic position in Agril. University	11	27.50	2	5.00	19	47.50
4 To start own business	12	30.00	8	20.00	2	5.00
5 To secure job in private company	6	15.00	12	30.00	6	15.00
6 To secure job in nationalised bank	5	12.50	11	27.50	7	17.50
7 To secure job in corporate sector	3	7.50	9	22.50	6	15.00
8 To secure job in Panchayat Raj Institutions	2	5.00	7	17.50	10	25.00
9 To secure job involuntary organisation	4	10.00	9	22.50	6	15.00
10 To start own consultancy in Agriculture	5	12.58	8	20.00	5	12.50
11 To undertake farming occupation	3	7.50	2	5.00	13	32.50
12 To secure job in I C A R	1	2.50	1	2.50	17	42.50
13 To secure job in central GOVT	2	5.00	7	17.50	12	30.00
14 To secure job in Cooperative societies	2	5.00	11	27.50	4	10.00
15 To secure job in Private Banks	7	17.50	8	20.50	2	5.00
16 To enter in Politics	11	27.50	5	12.50	-	-
17 To secure Sales and occupation	11	27.50	2	5.00	3	7.50
18 To become Business analyst	6	15.00	4	10.00	6	15.00
19 To become Agricultural University Scientist	6	15.00	11	27.50	-	-
20 To become farm Manager	2	5.00	7	17.50	12	30.00

The second order occupations preferred were to secure an administrative position in the Department of Agriculture (32.50

per cent) followed by securing a job in a private company and nationalised bank (27.50 per cent) each. The first preferred occupations were in the order of securing a administrative job in government departments (60.00 per cent) followed by securing a academic position in agricultural university (47.50 per cent) and to secure an administrative position in th Department of Agriculture (42.50 per cent) and job in ICAR (42.50 per cent).

Occupational Aspiration Preferences of Students (Overall)

A cursory look at Table 23 provides the information on the occupational aspiration preferences of students of different colleges at GKVK, Mandya and Shimoga. It is observed that most of the students preferred to enter into politics (23.30 per cent) followed by sales and business occupation (19.20 per cent) as their least preferred occupations. The second preferred occupations were to secure administrative position in the department of agriculture (32.50 per cent) followed by to secure job in cooperative societies (25.80 per cent) and in nationalised banks (22.50 per cent). The students preferred to secure the an administrative job in the government department (53.30 per cent) followed by securing an administrative position in the department of agriculture (33.30 per cent) and to secure an academic position in the agricultural university (31.70 per cent) as their top preferred occupation.

Table 23. Occupational Aspiration Preferences of Students of Different Agricultural Colleges

Sl. No. Job Preference	III Preference		II Preference		I Preference	
	No.	%	No.	%	No.	%
1. To secure the Administrative job in government departments	12	10.00	20	16.50	64	53.30
2. To secure administrative position in the Dept. of Agriculture	3	2.50	39	32.50	40	33.30
3. To secure academic position in Agricultural University	19	15.80	14	11.70	38	31.70

4. To start own consultancy in Agriculture	13	10.80	21	17.50	20	16.70
5. To secure job in I C A R	9	7.50	11	9.20	38	31.70
6. To start own business	23	19.20	24	20.00	18	15.00
7. To become Business analyst	12	10.00	16	13.30	18	15.00
8. To secure job in central GOVT	8	6.70	12	10.00	40	33.30
9. To secure job in Cooperative sector	9	7.50	31	25.80	11	9.20
10. To secure job in corporate sector	12	10.00	21	17.50	22	18.30
11. To undertake farming occupation	18	15.00	14	11.70	23	19.20
12. To secure job in nationalised bank	9	7.50	27	22.50	23	19.20
13. To secure job in Panchayat Raj Institutions	13	10.80	25	20.80	16	13.30
14. To enter in Politics	28	23.30	15	12.50	4	3.30
15. To secure job in Private Banks	15	12.50	22	18.30	9	7.50
16. To secure Sales and business occupation	23	19.20	14	11.70	11	9.20
17. To become Agricultural University Scientist	5	4.20	14	11.70	35	29.20
18. To become farm Manager	8	6.70	24	20.00	29	24.20
19. To secure job in voluntary organisations	17	14.20	19	15.80	20	16.70
20. To secure job in private company	19	15.80	25	20.80	18	15.00

Association between Personal and Socio-economic Characteristics and Aspirations of Students

Association between personal and socio-economic characteristics of students of different agricultural colleges of UAS, Bangalore, and their occupational level was tested using chi-square test and the results of the chi-square test is provided in Table 24 to 27.

Agricultural College, GKVK

The results of the chi-square and Kendall Tou test filled in Table 24 depicts a significant association between the education level of father the education level and mother, and the annual income level of respondents and their occupational aspiration level. It further denotes that the other variables such as age, sex, birthplace and native place, place of education, family type, sibling status, father's occupation, mother's occupation and academic performance level of students had no significant association with the occupational aspiration level.

Table 24. Association between Personal and Socio-economic Characteristics with Occupational Aspiration Level of GKVK Students.

(n=40)

Sl. No.	*Variables*	*Chi-square Value*	C
1	Age	3.210 Ns	0.273 Ns
2	Sex	0.618 Ns	0.123 Ns
3	Birthplace and native place	0.605 Ns	0.122 Ns
4	Place of education	2.704 Ns	0.252 Ns
5	Education level of father	6.521 *	0.374 *
6	Education level of mother	6.245 *	0.367 *
7	Father's occupation	2.608 Ns	0.348 Ns
8	Mother's occupation	2.704 Ns	0.252 Ns
9	Annual income	6.120 *	0.364 *
10	Family type	1.576 Ns	0.195 Ns
11	Sibling status	4.692 Ns	0.324 Ns
12	Academic performance	3.256 Ns	0.274 Ns

Ns-Non-significant

*-Significant at 5%

Agricultural College, Mandya

Table 25 indicates that there is a significant association between education level of father, birthplace and native place father's

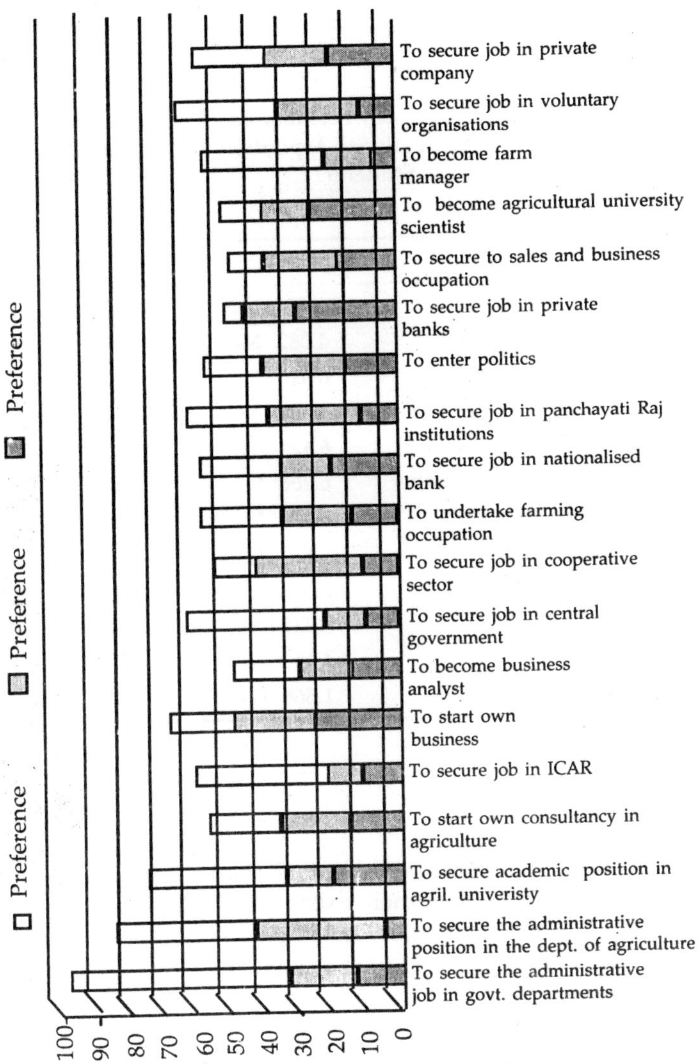

Figure 18. Occupational aspiration preferences of students of different Agricultural colleges

occupation and occupational aspiration level of students of Agricultural College, Mandya, as evidenced by the significant results of chi-square and Kendall Tou test. The other variables viz., age, sex, place of education, mother's occupation, family size, sibling status, annual income, and academic performance, had no significant association with the occupational aspiration level of students.

Table 25. Association between Personal and Socio-economic Characteristics with Occupational Aspiration level of Mandya Students.

(n=40)

Sl. No.	*Variables*	*Chi Square Value*	C
1	Age	4.744 Ns	0.326 Ns
2	Sex	4.082 Ns	0.304 Ns
3	Birthplace and native	6.316 *	0.369 *
4	Place of education	5.233 Ns	0.340 Ns
5	Education level of father	6.425 *	0.389 *
6	Education level of mother	6.266 *	0.344 *
7	Father's occupation	6.278 *	0.351 *
8	Mother's occupation	1.647 Ns	0.199 Ns
9	Annual income	0.059 Ns	0.038 Ns
10	Family type	3.335 Ns	0.277 Ns
11	Sibling status	4.135 Ns	0.306 Ns
12	Academic preference	1.566 Ns	0.194 Ns

Ns-Non-significant

*Significant at 5%

Agricultural College, Shimoga

The results of the chi-square and Kendall Tou test applied to the data in Table 26 reveals that there exists a significant association between the father's occupation and the education level of the mother of students and their occupational aspiration level. The results further indicated that the other variables, namely age, sex, birthplace and native place, place of education, education level, of father, annual income, family type, sibling status and academic performance had no significant association with the occupational aspiration level of students.

Table 26. Association between Personal and Socio-economic Characteristics with Occupational Aspiration Level of Shimoga Students

(n=40)

Sl. No.	*Variables*	*Chi Square Value*	*C*
1	Age	4.128 Ns	0.309 Ns
2	Sex	2.545 Ns	0.245 Ns
3	Birth and Native place	1.722 Ns	0.203 Ns
4	Place of education	3.180 Ns	0.271 Ns
5	Education level of father	4.181 Ns	0.308 Ns
6	Education level of mother	6.697 *	0.379 *
7	Father's occupation	6.316 *	0.367 *
8	Mother's occupation	1.260 Ns	0.175 Ns
9	Annual income	1.125 Ns	0.165 Ns
10	Family type	0.597 Ns	0.121 Ns
11	Sibling Status	5.364 Ns	0.344 Ns
12	Academic performance	2.012 Ns	0.219 Ns

Ns-Non-significant

*- Significant at 5 %

Overall Students

There is significant association among the education level of father, the education level of mother, father's occupation, mother's occupation and academic performance and occupational aspiration level of students in general as revealed by the results of chi-square and Kendall Tou test (Table 27). The variables namely age, sex, annual income, birth and native place, family type, sibling status and place of education of students and their occupational aspiration level had no significant association. The results of the significant association between dependent and independent variables is discussed hereunder.

Parents Education

The education level of father and mother has shown a significant association with the occupational aspirations of students. The higher the level of education of the parents the more likely they would be motivated to instil motivation for upward occupational mobility in their children. This is because the education widens the horizons of the parents which in turn affects the level of occupational aspirations of children. In other words, it reveal that the educational background of parents plays an important role in shaping the occupational aspirations of children. The present finding is in conformity with that of Sharma and Dantare (1995) and Pradhan (2002).

Table 27. Association between personal Socio-economics Characteristics with Occupational Aspiration of all Students

(n=120)

Sl. No.	*Variables*	*Chi Square Value*	C
1	Age	2.486 Ns	0.142 Ns
2	Sex	2.888 Ns	0.153 Ns
3	Birthplace and native place	2.289 Ns	0.137 Ns
4	Place of education	3.270 Ns	0.163 Ns
5	Education level of father	8.921 *	0.363 *
6	Education level of mother	6.939 *	0.355 *
7	Father's occupation	6.138 *	0.315 *
8	Mother's occupation	6.126 *	0.301 *
9	Annual income	0.732 Ns	0.078 Ns
10	Family type	0.520 Ns	0.066 Ns
11	Sibling status	2.084 Ns	0.131 Ns
12	Academic performance	6.603 *	0.315 *

Ns-Non-significant

*- Significant at 5 per cent

Parents Occupation

The observed chi-square for the data was significant at 5 per cent level. Thus it is clear that there existed significant associates between the occupational aspirations of students and occupation in which their father and mother were engaged in the finding, thus showing that by knowing the occupation of the parents one can predict the occupational aspiration of a child. It indicates that the higher occupation of parents, the higher will be the aspirations of respondents. The high occupation of parents provides a kind of environment which is responsible for high occupational aspirations of the adolescents. Sharma and Dantare (1995) reported similar findings.

Academic Performance

There existed a significant association between the academic performance and the level of occupational aspiration of students. It showed that those students who have a higher academic performance aspire for a higher level of aspiration than those who have a low academic performance. Similar findings were reported by Suryawanshi and Wattamwai (2003). Marine and Greenberger (1997) also reported that the academic achievement had a greater effect on the occupational aspiration of students of Pennsylvania.

Sources of Information Utilised for Job Placements

The data on sources of information consulted by students of different colleges for job placements is provided in Table 28. It is observed from the table that a majority of the students in general used mass media sources to a maximum extent followed by informal and formal sources. Among the mass media sources, most of the students used websites (67.50 per cent) followed by newspapers (62.50 per cent), television (35.00 per cent) and journals (20.00 per cent). Friends (66.66 per cent), parents (31.66 per cent) and relatives (27.50 per cent) among informal sources and university placement cell (30.83 per cent), Agricultural officers (26.66 per cent) and consultants (19.16 per cent) among formal sources were utilised by majority of the students in general.

With respect to Agricultural College, GKVK, websites (72.50 per cent) and journals (17.5 per cent) were popular among mass media sources. Friends (55.00 per cent), parents (22.50 per cent) and relatives among informal sources and university placement cell (27.50 per cent), consultants (17.50 per cent) and agricultural officers (15.00 per cent) among formal sources were consulted by most of the students for job placement. Regarding Agricultural College, Mandya, the most utilised sources by the students were website (62.50 per cent), newspaper (62.50 per cent) and television (52.50 per cent) among mass media sources, friends

(75.00 per cent), relatives (45.00 per cent), and neighbours (32.50 per cent) among informal sources and university placement cell (45.00 per cent), consultants (32.50 per cent) and agricultural officers (35.00 per cent) among formal sources. A large majority of the students of Agricultural College, Shimoga, consulted websites (70.00 per cent), newspapers (67.50 per cent), and television (27.50 per cent), among mass media sources. Friends (70.00 per cent), parents (40.00 per cent) and Neighbors (27.50 per cent), among informal sources and agricultural officers (30.00 per cent) and university placement cell (20.00 per cent) among formal sources were consulted by a good number of students for job placement.

Table 28. Sources of Information Utilised for Job Placement

(n=120)

Sl. No	*Source*	*Agril. College GKVK*		*Agril. College Mandya*		*Agril. College Shimoga*		*Total*	
A	*Informed source*	*No.*	*%*	*No.*	*%*	*No.*	*%*	*No.*	*%*
1	Friends	22	55.00	30	75.00	28	70.00	80	66.66
2	Relatives	6	15.00	18	45.00	9	22.50	33	27.50
3	Neighbours	3	7.500	13	32.50	11	27.50	27	22.50
4	Parents	9	22.50	13	32.50	16	40.00	38	31.66
B	*Mass Media Sources*								
5	Websites	29	72.50	25	62.50	28	70.00	81	67.50
6	Newspapers	22	55.00	25	62.50	27	67.50	75	62.50
7	Television	10	25.00	21	52.50	11	27.50	42	35.00
8	Journals	7	17.50	6	15.50	11	27.50	24	20.00
9	Radio	2	5.00	5	12.50	8	20.00	15	12.50
C	*Formal Source*								
10	University placement cell	11	27.50	18	45.00	8	20.00	37	30.83
11	Agril. officers	6	15.00	14	35.00	12	30.00	32	26.66
12	Consultants	7	17.50	13	32.50	3	7.50	23	19.16
13	Bank officer	1	2.50	10	25.00	3	7.50	23	19.16

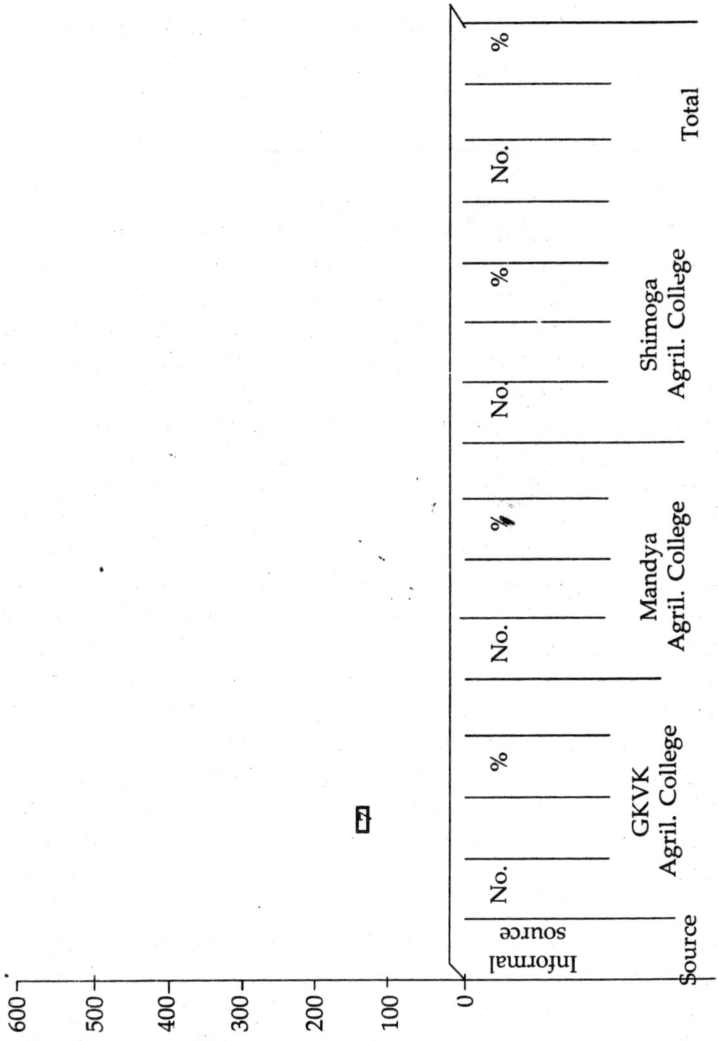

Figure 17. Sources of Information Utilized for Job Placement

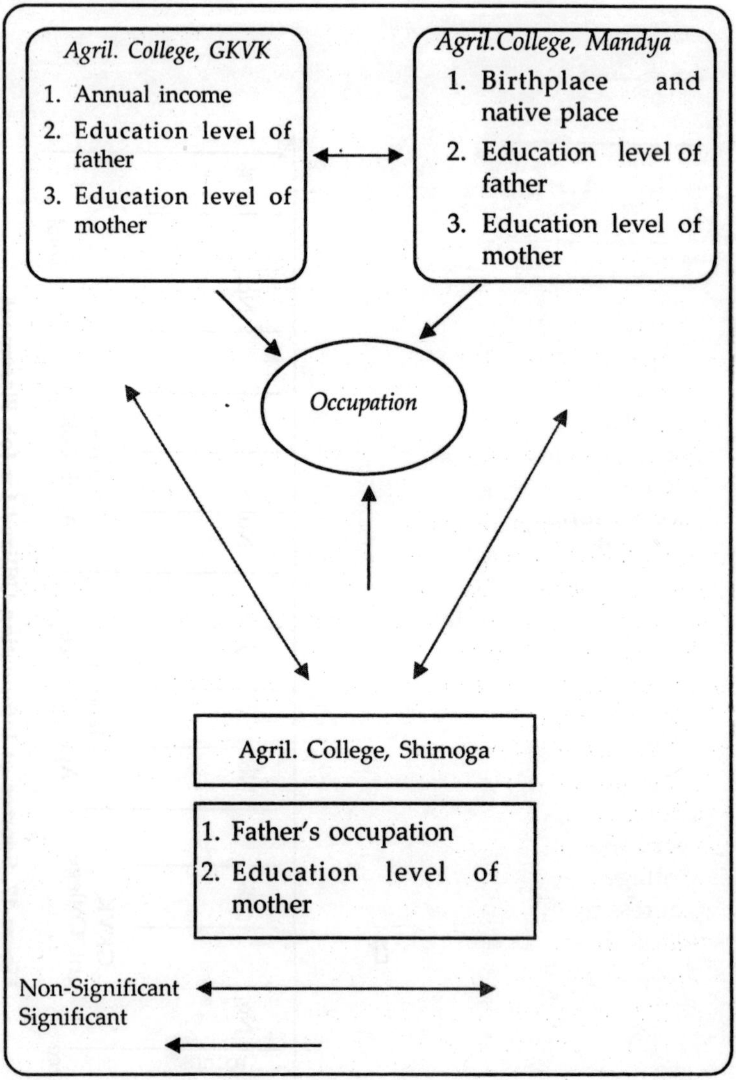

Figure 18. Empirical Model of the Study

4

Agricultural Extension Education

Agricultural extension work has a venerable, albeit largely unrecorded, history. It is a significant social innovation, an important force in agricultural change, which has been created and recreated, adapted and developed over the centuries. Its evolution extends over nearly four thousand years, although its modem forms are largely a product of the past two centuries. Today, the organisations and personnel engaged in agricultural extension encompass a diverse range of socially sanctioned and legitimate activities which seek to enlarge and improve the abilities of farm people to adopt more appropriate and often new practices and to adjust to changing conditions and socialite needs.

The word "extension" was first time used in Britain in 1840 in the form of "University Extension" or "Extension of the University". In 1850, William Sewell of Britain used it in his report entitled "suggestions for the extension of the university". But, this word was first used in a practical way by James Stuart of Trinity College, Cambridge University in 1867-68, when he was addressing "Women Association and Working Men's Clubs" of North England. Again in 1871, he appealed to the officials of the Cambridge University to establish extension centres under the supervision of university, so that these centres can be used as a platform to deliver lecture to the people. His effort in this field was responsible for him being called "Father of University Extension". In a formal way, Cambridge University in 1873, London University in 1876 and Oxford University in 1878 developed extension system, which worked among people. In 1880, his work came to be known as "extension movement. " In the eighth decade of the 19th century, the word "extension" was used in the form of extension education in U.S.A.

According to Webster's dictionary the term "extension" means "branch of a university for student who cannot attend the University properly". In other words, the word 'extension' is used in the context which signifies an out of school system of education." In 1862 President Roosevelt established a "county commission" under the chairmanship of Liverty Hydevelle. Its objectives were: (a) how to stop migration of rural people to cities and (b) how to engage rural people in agricultural and rural development programmes. It was due to the fact that industrial development is not possible without agricultural development so, maximum people must live in the villages and help in the agricultural development. County commission in its report stated that firstly, there is vast difference between rural and urban life and this should be lessened. It further stated that the standard of living of rural people can be uplifted permanently only when they themselves make an effort in this direction. Secondly, in order to encourage people to take initiative, it is prerequisite that the change in the field of knowledge, understanding, skill and attitude should be brought about.

In order to implement the above recommendations educational work has to be taken upon. Therefore, county commission recommended the establishment of an institution, which can organise out of school education. Keeping this in mind Smith Leaver Act (1914) was passed and this Act led to the integration of cooperative extension service according to which out of school education was organised. As a result, rural people were able to bring about developments and progress in farming and housing. This type of education comes to be known as "agricultural extension education".

Extension education is an applied behavioural science, the knowledge of which is applied to bring about desirable changes in the behavioural complex of human beings usually through various strategies and programmes of change and by applying the latest scientific and technological innovations. Extension education has now developed as a full-fledged discipline, having its own philosophy, objectives, principles, methods and techniques which must be understood by every extension worker and others connected with the rural development. It might be mentioned here that extension education, its principles, methods and techniques are applicable not only to agriculture but also to veterinary and animal husbandry, dairying, home science, health, family planning, etc. Based upon its application and use, various nomenclatures have been given to it, such as agricultural extension, veterinary and animal husbandry extension, dairy extension, home science extension, public health extension, and family planning extension.

Concepts of Extension Education

Some important concepts of extension education are presented below:

i) *Extension*: The word extension is mostly used for Extension Education.

ii) *The basic concept of extension is that it is education*: Means production of desirable change in human behaviour, which includes knowledge, attitude and skill.

iii) *Extension work*: It means the whole structure of extension work. It includes the process of extension education i.e. the process of teaching and learning. Besides the process, in extension work are included organisation, administration, supervision, finances as well as the progrmmes for the overall development.

iv) *Extension service*: It means an organisation and/or a programme for the welfare and development, which employs the extension educational process for the implementation of programme. It is thus same as that of extension work except that in extension service there has been greater emphasis on service.

v) *Extension job*: The job of extension in agriculture and home science is to assist people engaged in farming and home-making to utilise their own resources more effectively and those that are available to them, in solving the current problems and in meeting the changing economic and social conditions.

vi) *Extension educational process*: The extension process is working with the people with their immediate needs and interests, which can make available additional occupation, make improvement in the socio-economic status, better home-management and expedite welfare of the rural people.

vii) *Methods of education*: Education must be conceived as a life long learning process. Human beings learn mainly by three methods: (a) through informal education; (b) formal education; and (c) non-formal education.

   a) *Informal education:* It is the never-ending process by which an individual learns through daily experiences and exposure to environment at home—at work, from friends, radio, television, papers and books etc.

   b) *Formal education*: It is institutionalised, chronologically graded and well-structured system of education, which starts from schooling to the higher education.

   c) *Non-formal education*: It has been a well organised, systematic educational activity that is carried on outside formal educational system in order to provide certain selected type of learning to the selected group of individuals which include adults, young as well as the children. Included in the non-formal education are subjects on the various aspects of agriculture and related fields, like training progrmmes for farmers, farm-women and rural youth. Training has been provided on skill development of various aspects, which may help in generation of employment. Farm-women clubs, self help groups, Home Science activities such as health, nutrition, childcare, sanitation and fruit and vegetable preservation etc.

viii) Technology assessment for sustainable agriculture and rural development is defined here as a comprehensive approach to examine the actual or potential impact of technology applications on certain sustainability issues and second order consequences and to facilitate the development and use of technological interventions according to location-specific constraints and objectives.

ix) Technology transfer was taken to mean a system under which various inter-related components of technology, namely, "hardware" (materials such as a variety), "software" (technique, know-how, information), human-ware (human ability), "orga-ware" (organisational aspects) and the final product (including marketing) are rendered accessible to the end-users (farmers).

x) *Appropriate technology*: Appropriate technology refers to a technology package, which must be technically feasible, economically viable, socially acceptable, environment-friendly, consistent with household endowments, and relevant to the needs of farmers. Technologies are subject to adjustment, change and evolution.

xi) *Sustainability:* The underlying definition is the one adopted by the FAO in 1988, sustainable development is the management and conservation of the natural resource base, and the orientation of technological and institutional change in such a manner as to ensure the attainment and continued satisfaction of human needs for present and future generations. Such sustainable development (in the agriculture, forestry, animal and fisheries sectors) conserve land, water, plant and animal genetic resources, is environmentally non-degrading, technically appropriate, economically viable and socially acceptable.

Nature of Extension Education

Extension education is an education and it is bringing a desirable change in behaviour (knowledge, skills and attitudes) of rural people to improve their social, economic and psychological status.

The features of extension education are described in the following points:

i) Extension education is a system in which youth both male and female, adult people and women are encouraged to work for their own development and prosperity.

ii) Extension education is an informal system of education for all rural people.

iii) Extension education brings required change among the people of rural area.

iv) Extension education helps only those people who are prepared to help themselves.

v) It educates people as to how to achieve their target.

vi) Extension education educates people through "learning by doing" and "seeing is believing".

vii) Extension education is a two-way system of education. It brings scientific knowledge to the rural people and conveys the problems of rural people to the scientific institution for solution.

viii) Extension education works together with the rural people, and thereby helps people to bring prosperity to their home, family, society, community and country.

ix) Extension education helps in personality development, raising standard of living of people, developing local leaders and development of society and country.

x) Extension education is a continuous educational process, which goes on between teachers and learners. In this both teacher and learner benefit and learn from each other.

Extension Education Process

Extension is a continuous educational process. Primarily, in an effective extension education programme, the following five stages are included:

i) *Study of situation and problem*: At this stage Extension Personnel should collect all information about farmers, i.e., farmers education, interest, requirement, way of thinking, viewpoint and social status. Information related to physical condition, i.e., type of soil, types of land, market, cropping method, size of land, family status, community service, communication facilities etc. should be collected and study of local, social, national and international problems should also be undertaken. Extension personnel should analyse these factors on the basis of "What they are" and "What they ought to be". Only after analysing all these problems the solution should be considered.

ii) *Objectives and solution*. At this stage, objectives of Extension Education should be according to above-mentioned requirements. In drafting the objectives the Extension Personnel should keep in mind the following points:

a) Objectives should be limited and extremely important.

b) Participation of rural people should be compulsorily included.

c) Objectives should be able to bring about desired change in human behaviour.

iii) *Teaching plan of work*: There are two main points in this third stage: (a) what should be and (b) how it should be. In this stage, extension methods should be selected and all the conditions necessary for learning process should be created so that the people can easily learn it to solve their problem and bring about change in their behaviour. How the Extension Personnel selects the extension methods will reflect his true capabilities and worth.

iv) *Evaluation*: At this stage, all the work done until now is evaluated and it is seen that whether the objectives were properly chosen and how they are executed. From this we can figure out whether we are going in right direction or not. The success and failure of extension educational programme depends on this stage of evaluation. The facts should be analysed without any bias during evaluation.

v) *Reconsideration*: If our evaluation results indicate that our aim and objectives are not fulfilled and that we have to do the work again than we should repeat educational process from first step to the last step.

In this way, the extension educational process continuously goes on till the all-round development of people is achieved.

Objectives of Extension Education

The main aim of extension education is to bring about all-round development of rural people. In this all-round development educational, social, economic and political developments are included. The first aim of Extension Education is to bring change in the behaviour, in work capacity and in attitude in wider context. The second aim of Extension Education like social, economic and political change is automatically achieved by bringing about above mentioned educational changes. How to achieve this aim is known as objectives. In this context the objectives of Extension Education are as following:

i) To increase the net income of farmers by more production and proper marketing system.

ii) To raise the standard of living of rural people.

iii) Development of rural areas.

iv) To increase the facilities for social, cultural and entertainment programmes for rural people.
v) To develop rural leadership.
vi) To develop the feeling of self-dependence among rural people.
vii) To provide educational and health facilities in rural areas.
viii) To develop feeling of patriotism and love for society by developing civic sense among rural people.
ix) To encourage rural people to participate in community programmes.
x) To train rural youth for development works.

SCOPE OF EXTENSION EDUCATION

Extension work will speed up only when the development of factors related to it i.e., (a) man environment; (b) basic structures (gram panchayat, village school and cooperative societies) will be undertaken.

i) *Personal development of people:*
   a) Increase in agricultural production so that standard of living can be raised.
   b) Facility for rural industry related knowledge.
   c) Facility for advance techniques/methods.
   d) Development of co-industries like animal husbandry, poultry, goats and pigery farming etc.
   e) Training the people for development of agriculture and rural industry.
   f) Proper educational facilities for rural people.
   g) To inculcate self-confidence, self-dependence and desire to work themselves among rural people.
ii) *Development of environment of people:*
   a) Arrangement of family-education.
   b) Eradication of prevalent social evils.
   c) Development of democratic ways.
   d) Maximum use of available resources for community work.
   e) Management of rural hygiene and environment.

iii) *Development of basic institutions:*

a) To develop confidence and respect for these institutions.

b) To develop feeling of responsibility among the people.

c) To increase cooperation of maximum number of people.

Principles of Extension Education

Principles of extension education are simple, easy, educative and moral. Generally principles of extension are as follows:

i) *Principle of need and interest*: Extension work is self-educative process. To make extension work more effective, it is necessary that it should be done according to peoples' needs and interest. Extension worker should take notice of local peoples' needs. As this will generate interest of the people which in turn will lead to their cooperation in extension work

ii) *Principle of cooperation and participation*: Principle of cooperation and participation is very important in extension education. Ultimately without the cooperation of people the work cannot be successful and desired result cannot be achieved. The first task of extension education is the cooperation of people and their participation in work. People should realise that the task of extension education is their own task. Participation in extension work generates confidence among people for the work. It is not essential that all the members of the society should participate but extension worker should try for maximum participation of people.

iii) *Principle of cultural difference*: Rural people have high faith in traditional customs and values. Therefore, extension worker should be aware of what the rural people know, Think and also about their belief. Cultural changes should be gradual and in accordance with the cultural status of people. It is very difficult to achieve success in extension work by neglecting their views and cultural behaviour.

iv) *Principle of applied science and democratic approach*: Extension Education is based upon democratic principles. It is based on discussions and suggestions. Discussions are held with the people on actual condition so that they participate in work. Extension worker provide practical look to the scientific inventions so that farmers can easily adopt them in their farm.

v) *Principle of learning by doing:* According to this principle farmers are encouraged to learn by doing the work themselves and by participating themselves. When a person does a work he gains practical knowledge and experiences the difficulties. Extension worker is able to understand the problems and provide proper guidance to the farmers and thus, they are able to receive proper information.

vi) *Principle of trained specialists*: It is very difficult that extension personnel should be knowledgeable about all problems. Therefore, it is necessary that specialists should impart training to the farmers from time to time.

vii) *Adaptability principles in use of extension teaching methods*: Extension worker should have knowledge of extension methods so that they can select proper method according to the condition. Teaching methods should be flexible so that they can be properly applied on people according to then age groups, educational background, economic standard and gender. In extension education two or more methods should be applied according to principle of adaptability.

viii) *Principle of leadership*: The participation or inclusion of local leaders in extension programmes is the only criteria for assessing the success or failure of any extension work. Local leader is the best medium for dissemination of new ideas in rural area. According to Ensminger. "No Extension worker can be successful till he receives the cooperation of local leader of the village." It is very necessary for extension worker to select the proper leader. By selecting a proper leader, extension worker's half work is considered to be done as such, proper precautions should be undertaken to choose the leader.

ix) *Principle of whole family*: In Extension Education, principle of whole family is of utmost importance. Family is a part of the community, so there should be development of each member of the family and extension education should be for each and every member of the family, i.e., boys, girls, male and female, then only success can be achieved.

x) *Principle of satisfaction*: If people are not interested in extension work then there is no possibility that extension work can be carried on for a long time. In a democratic structure/set-up people cannot be run in a mechanised way. They should derive full satisfaction from extension work. Extension worker should give priority to those work in which there is scope for immediate benefits. Primary satisfaction is very helpful for the future of extension work.

xi) *Principle of evaluation*: It is necessary to evaluate the extension work after a certain period so that merits and demerits of extension work can come to light and necessary changes be brought about. Evaluation generates confidence in people.

xii) *Principle of neutrality*: Extension worker should never take interest in local politics. If he will not behave in this manner then lots of difficulties in extension work will arise. Therefore, remaining neutral is more beneficial. Extension worker should never express his special affection or hatred towards any person.

xiii) *Principle of encouragement*: In extension work, principles of encouragement have great importance. Under pressure no work can be done in extension programme, for this active workers in this field should be encouraged so that they participate and enthusiastically remain active.

Importance of Extension Education

Extension education aims to bring necessary change in the beliefs or views of people. It is an educational process by which capabilities among people are developed to understand their problems and resources. It is utilised to make scientific methods available to the rural people, so that they can raise their agricultural production and their standard of living. In India, the aim of extension education is community development, which is possible only by bringing change in the behaviour complex of rural people. Extension education plays major role in bringing desirable change in rural people. In rural development or community development through extension education, the following functions should be performed:

i) *Providing knowledge*: It implies bringing change in a person's present knowledge by providing information about latest developmental works, like, providing knowledge about new species. If a person is not aware of development works then information about it is imparted through training programmes.

ii) *Changing attitude*: The positive change in attitude of people towards the information given to them about latest developmental works should be brought about if a person believes that it is right for him then he will surely adopt it. In the same way there should be attitudinal change in the extension worker so that he can be able to increase the speed of development in the area by spreading new technique.

iii) *Developing skills*: Whatever work a person does, he should do so by adopting new technologies, which minimise his time, money and hardship and increases production and his income in proportionate way. Therefore, change in skills of people should be brought about. In similar way, there should be change in skill of extension personnel so that he could practically exhibit the new technique in the area and people can easily understand.

iv) *Changing goals*: If a person's aim is to grow only two crops in the field then he should be counselled that he can grow more than two crops in his fields and in place of food crops he should grow cash crops in some areas. This way he will have more profit and can aim for high crop production. Similarly, extension personnel should aim to spread this new technique in his area at certain period.

v) *Changing actions*: Extension worker should bring change in action of the people. People should be told to immediately make plans about the implementation of new techniques, which have been brought to their knowledge. In exactly the same way, extension personnel should plan the extension work immediately.

vi) *Building confidence*: There should be change in confidence of the people that by adopting new techniques there will be definite increase in their net income. Similarly extension worker should have confidence that his extension work will definitely bring welfare of the society.

vii) *Developing leaders*: Extension worker should develop permanent leadership in village, who can adopt new technology and help in spreading the new technology.

viii) *Developing rural groups and institutions*: In rural areas, collective change occurs very enthusiastically, therefore, it is necessary to develop rural groups in villages. By proper development of gram panchayat, co-operative institutions and other institutions, greater cooperation is achieved in rural development, therefore, they should be developed.

Qualities of Extension Worker

Extension worker is like a teacher, philosopher, leader, guide and colleague for the community and on the basis of his special qualities he is able to carry on developmental programme successfully. It is undoubtedly true to say that the success and failure of development programmes depend upon the qualities of extension worker. Now we will do realistic study of those necessary qualities and capabilities of extension worker. By extension worker we mean a man who is the last chain of extension organisation, who while living in the midst of the community, propagates his programmes. An extension worker should have the following qualities to be successful in his career:

i) *Sound knowledge*: The work of extension worker is to introduce villagers to new ideas and to bring change in their behaviour. But, he cannot be successful in this work unless he himself is aware of new technologies. Only after having full and complete knowledge about latest techniques/technologies, he will be able to impress the people.

ii) *Explicitness*: Extension worker lives alone in the village and he has to provide appropriate solution to the problems of the people. Therefore extension worker should be capable of taking prompt action and providing explicit solution.

Opposite trait in extension worker will create disbelief and disappointment among people.

iii) *Foresightedness*: Extension work is a continuous process, therefore, extension worker should have foresightedness to know which type of work will bring, what kind of result and what will be its impact on the people. He should also know which work should be given priority in order to achieve long lasting benefit.

iv) *Service attitude*: The mentality of extension worker should be filled with servitude. As far as possible at every stage, he should perform his duties and should not exert his rights. Due to this mental attitude, other people will also take interest in social welfare programme and new leadership will emerge and help voluntary in extension work.

v) *Enthusiasm*: A body without enthusiasm is like a cadaver. Person who himself is not motivated, self-confident and aware, cannot convince others to follow his path. Enthusiasm is sure way for success. It enhances personality of extension worker. It is also relevant here to mention that over-enthusiasm is harmful.

vi) *Honesty*: Wherever there is a question of behaviour and policy, people should practise honesty and truthfulness. Extension work is a practical work in which definite policy is adopted through which new motivation emerge in the community.

vii) *Organising capacity*: The success of extension work depends on two main factors: (a) Development of power of motivation. (b) Capability to organise people. Power of motivation develops naturally but capability to organise people is very important for doing any kind of work. The proper utilisation of money, labour and other resources of people is possible only when all these different factors are properly organised.

The role of extension worker while living among rural people is to bring necessary change in individual and collective behaviour and motivating them. For this, extension worker is required to have knowledge about psychological factors, extension related training and technological knowledge.

Learning and Teaching in Extension

Extension is an educational process for bringing about the maximum number of desirable changes among the people, which involves both learning and teaching and needs some tools or methods commonly known as extension-teaching methods. It is, therefore, necessary here to understand what is meant by learning, teaching and extension methods.

'Learning' is the process by which an individual, through his own activity, attains a change in his behaviour. It is an active process on the part of the learner. The essential role of an extension worker is to create effective 'learning situations'. An effective learning situation requires the following essential elements:

i) An instructor (an extension worker, e.g. an extension officer or a village-level worker).

ii) Learners (the farmers, the farm women and the youth).

iii) Subject-matter (the recommended improved practices, such as the seeds of high-yielding varieties, fertilisers, balanced diet, etc.)

iv) Teaching material, such as a flannel-board, a black-board, charts, models, samples, slides, film strips, etc.

v) Physical facilities, such as sitting accomodation, good visibility, etc.

The extension worker should skillfully manipulate the elements of the learning situation and provide satisfactory learning experiences for the people. The farmer, the farmer women or the farm youth are the focal points in the learning situation. The main aim of an extension worker is to bring about a change in this behaviour of the people with the help of a judicious combination and use of different elements. All the teaching should be carried out according to the needs and resources of the local community or group.

Teaching is the process of arranging situations in which the things to be learnt are brought to the notice of the learners, their interest is developed and desire aroused, i.e. they are stimulated to action. For example, if we want to teach the farmers the use and advantages of chemical fertilisers, we do this by conducting demonstrations on their fields, showing them how the fertilisers are applied, and compare the yield of the fertilised crop with that of the crop to which no fertilisers has ben applied. After seeing the beneficial effect of a fertilisers, the farmer is convinced and motivated to action and starts using fertilisers regularly.

When extension education is put into action for educating the rural people, it does not remain formal education. In that sense, there are several differences between the two. Some of these differnces are:

Table 1. Differences between formal and extension education

Formal education	*Extension education*
1. The teacher starts with theory and works up to practicals.	1. The teacher (extension worker) starts with practicals and may take up theory later on.
2. Students study subjects.	2. Farmers study problems.
3. Students must adapt themselves to the fixed curriculum offered.	3. It has no fixed curriculum or course of study and the farmers help to formulate the curriculum.
4. Authority rests with the teacher.	4. Authority rests with the farmers.
5. Class attendance is compulsory.	5. Participation is voluntary.
6. Teacher instructs the students.	6. Teacher teaches and also learns from the farmers.
7. Teaching is only through instructors.	7. Teaching is also through local leaders.
8. Teaching is mainly vertical.	8. Teaching is mainly horizontal.
9. The teacher has more or less homogeneous audience.	9. The teacher has a large and heterogeneous audience.
10. It is rigid.	10. It is flexible.
11. It has all pre-planned and pre-decided programmes.	11. It has freedom to develop programmes locally and they are based on the needs and expressed desires of the people.
12. It is more theoretical.	12. It is more practical and intended for immediate application in the solution of problems.

Extension teaching Methods

The extension-teaching methods are the tools and techniques used to create situations in which communication can take place between the rural people and the extension workers. They are the methods of extending new knowledge and skills to the rural people by drawing their attention towards them, arousing their interest and helping them to have a successful experience of the new practice. A proper understanding of these methods and their selection for a particular type of work are necessary.

Classification

According to use

One way of classifying the extension methods is according to their use and nature of contact. In other words, whether they are used for contacting people individually, in groups or *in masses*. Based upon the nature of contact, they are divided into individual, group and mass-contact methods.

Individual-contact methods. Extension methods under this category provide opportunities for face-to-face or person-to-person contact between the rural people and the extension workers. These methods are very effective in teaching new skills and creating goodwill between farmers and the extension workers.

Group-contact methods. Under this category, the rural people or farmers are contacted in a group which usually consists of 20 to 25 persons. These groups are usually formed around a common interest. These methods also involve a face-to-face contact with the people and provide an opportunity for the exchange of ideas, for discussions on problems and technical recommendations and finally for deciding the future course of action.

Mass or community-contact methods. An extension worker has to approach a large number of people for disseminating a new informaton and helping them to use it. This can be done through mass-contact methods conveniently. These methods are more useful for making people aware of the new agricultural technology quickly.

Important extension-teaching methods under these three categories are listed in the following table.

Table 2. Classification of extension-teaching methods according to their use

Individual contacts	Group contacts	Mass contacts
Farm and home visits	Method demonstration and result demonstration	Bulletins
Office calls	National demonstration leader-training meetings	Leaflets
Telephone calls	Conferences and discussion meetings and workshops	Circular letters and radio
Personal letters	Field trips	Television, exhibitions, fairs, posters

According to form

Extension-teaching methods are also classified according to their forms, such as written, spoken and audiovisual. Some of the important methods under each of these 3 categories are given in table 3.

Table 3. Classification of extension-teaching methods according to their form

Written	Spoken	Objective or visual
Bulletins	General and special meetings	Result demonstration
Leaflets, articles	Farm and home visits	Demonstration posters
Personal letters	Official calls	Motion-pictures, charts
Circular letters	Telephone calls, radio	Slides, models, exhibits

A brief description of some of the extension methods which are commonly used by extension workers is given below.

- *Farm and home visits.* Farm and home visits constitute the direct or face-to-face contact by an extension worker with the farmer or the members of his family. During these visits, information is exchanged or discussed. The visits may be to get acquainted with the problems of the farmers, or to organisational purposes. Such visits provide an opportunity for a two-way communication.
- *Result demonstration.* Result demonstration is an educational test to prove the advantages of recommended practices and to demonstrate their applicability to the local condition. It is conducted by a farmer under the direct

supervision of an extension worker. It is designed to teach others, in addition to the person who conducts the demonstration. It helps the farmers to learn by seeing and doing. This method can be used to show the supoeriority of practices, such as the use of fertilisers, insecticides and pesticides and high yielding varieties of seeds.

- *Method demonstration.* It is used to show the technique of doing things or carrying out new practices, e.g. preparing a nursery-bed, treating seed with insecticides and fungicides, line-sowing, taking a soil sample, grafting fruit trees, etc. This method is usually used for groups of people.
- *National demonstrations.* National demonstrations are the "first-line demonstrations," conducted by researchers on the farmers' fields to show how production can be increased per unit of area and per unit of time. These demonstrations usually include the system of multiple cropping and the use of high-yielding varieties, along with the best package of practices. They were first initiated on a modest scale in 1965 and have now become a part of the agricultural production programme in the country.
- *Group discussions.* All the farmers cannot be contacted by extension workers individually because of their large number. It is convenient and feasible to contact them in groups. This method is commonly known as group discussion. It is used to encourage and stimulate the people to learn more about the problems that concern the community through discussion. It is a good method of involving the local people in developing local leadership and in deciding on a plan of action in a democratic way.
- *Exhibitions.* An exhibition is a systematic display of information, actual specimens, models, posters, photographs, and charts, etc., in a logical sequence. It is organised for arousing the interest of the visitors in the things displayed. It is one of the best media for reaching a large number of people, especially illiterate and semi-illiterate people. Exhibitions are used for a wide range of topics, such as planning a model village, demonstrating improved irrigation practices, soil conservation methods, showing high-yielding varieties of seeds and plants, new

agricultural implements and the best products of village industries.

- *General meetings.* These are usually held for passing on certain information to the people for future action. Extension workers give lectures to the people on certain pre-selected items of work, such as the celebration of *Van mahotsav*, a national festival.
- *Campaigns.* Campaigns are used to focus the attention of the people on a particular problem, e.g. rat control, village sanitation and plant protection, the production of *rabi* crops and family planning. Through this method, the maximum number of farmers can be reached in the shortest possible time. It builds up community confidence and involves the people emotionally in a programme.
- *Tours and field days.* Conducted tours for farmers are used to convince them and to provide them with an opportunity of seeing the results of new practices, demonstration skills, new implements etc. and to give them an idea regarding the suitability and application of these things in their own area. Such tours may also be arranged to enable the rural people to visit places and institutions connected with the problems of rural life, such as research institutions, training institutions, agricultural universities, model villages, areas of advanced developments, leading private farms, exhibitions, and agricultural and cattle fairs.
- *Printed matter.* Newspapers, magazines, bulletins, leaflets, folders, pamphlets and wall news-sheets are another set of mass media for communicating information to a large number of literate people. They are used for communicating general and specific information on a programme of technology or a practice. Small folders, leaflets and pamphlets are used to give specific recommendations about a practice, such as the use of fertilisers, vegetable cultivation, green-manuring and the growing of individual crops, e.g. wheat, barley, gram and sugarcane.
- *Radio.* It is a mass medium of communication and can reach a large number of people at any given time involving the least expense. Extension workers use the radio for

communicating information on new methods and techniques, giving timely information about the control of croppests and diseases, weather, market news, etc. For this purpose, talks, group discussions, folk-songs, dialogues and dramas are usually organised. There are 38 stations of All-India Radio broadcasting regular rural programmes.

- *Television* It is one of the most powerful media of communication. It has come into vogue only in the recent years. It combines both audio and visual impact and is very suitable for the dissemination of agricultural information. It is more useful in teaching how to do a specific job. A beginning has ben made in India for using this medium for development programmes since 1967, and it is expected that its use will become more extensive in the coming years.
- *Motion-pictures (movies).* Movies are an effective tool for arousing interest among the people, because they involve seeing, hearing, and action. They are the most suitable medium for drawing bigger audience. A film show can be followed by a discussion with the villagers.

Visual Aids

Visual aids are the tools of teaching through the sense of sight. They are supporting materials and they alone cannot generate learning. They should be considered only a tool that helps to do a job in a better way.

Visual aids are of different types. The following are the more commonly used ones in India:

i) Posters
ii) Flannel-graphs
iii) Flash cards
iv) Puppets
v) Slides and film-strips
vi) Models
vii) Bulletin boards
viii) photographs
ix) Black-boards
x) Cultural programmes

Posters. A good poster creates awareness and interest among the people. It inspires and takes people towards action. It consists of 3 main parts. The first usually announces the purpose or the approach, the second sets out conditions, and the third recommends action. A poster should be bold enough to attract attention of the people, and should communicate only one idea at a time. It should have simple letters which are clear and forceful.

Flannel-graphs. Flannel-graphs serve as a good teaching aid. When a piece of sandpaper is fixed to the back of a picture, a photograph, a letter, etc. They can be made to adhere easily to a piece of thick flannel cloth, fixed on a board. They are used as an aid for group methods like informal talks or lectures.

Flash cards. Flash cards are a set of small compact cards approximately 30 to 45 cm. In size, and are used to bring home an idea, such as the benefits of a smokeless *chulha,* the cultivation of hybrid maize, compost-making and other practices. Pictures on the theme are drawn on these cards in a logical sequence which are flashed before the audience. Upon seeing them, the villagers are able to follow a story more easily.

Puppets. Puppets are very popular and especially suitable for village situations. Puppet shows can be effectively organised to gather the rural people. For a puppet show, a short story, brief scenes and quick dialogues are necessary. Such shows can teach a lesson about health, literacy, agriculture.

Slides. A slide is a transparent picture or photograph in an individual mount. For viewing the image, the picture is projected through a slide-projector which brings the enlarged image into focus on a screen. Slides are excellent aids of illustrating talks and showing people concrete activities and aspects of development. They can be effectively used to show different situations and methods of carrying out an activity. They can be arranged in a series for giving an illustrated talk on improved agricultural practices, cultivation of crops, etc.

Film-strips. They are a series of black-and-white or coloured pictures depicting a single idea, and instead of being individually mounted are printed on a single length of strip of 35-mm film. Such strips can be shown to an audience of about a 100 people. The additional advantage in using the film-strips is that the film can be stopped anytime during the show to explain or discuss a difficult or interesting point.

Models. Models create a sense of realisation in a person. Models of new farm equipments, compost pits and sanitation devices and animals are mostly prepared for those people who are not in a position to see them in the actual form. They are used to create interest, promote understanding and influence the people to adopt a certain practice.

Bulletin-boards. A bulletin-board can serve the purpose of making announcements, displaying events of short duration and photographs of local activities. The information should be written in simple language.

Photographs. They are a very simple visual aid. Good photographs show some action and catch the feelings and emotions of the people. They are so arranged that they tell a story. They are displayed on a bulletin-board at a common meeting-place where a large number of people can see them. They should be clear and bold in composition with proper captions.

Black-boards. They provide a writing and drawing surface for chalk. They are usually used in schools, colleges and meeting places. They make possible the use of sketches, drawings, words, symbols of a combination of them to emphasise a point. Black-boards are most useful in group-teaching methods.

Cultural programmes. Local cultural programmes, such as folk-songs and dramas, are used as an effective medium of communicating the message of development programmes. Dramatisation of a theme or story creates a lively interest among the audience. Folk-songs and dances related to the subjects of local interest and importance, when acted on the stage, bring them home more forcefully.

For an effective use of extension-teaching methods, it is not enough to know these methods and their techniques. What is more important is the appropriate selection of a method or combination of methods for a particular situation. In fact, when a farmer is exposed to a new idea several times by different methods or a combination of methods, he is likely to accept it more quickly. Farmers learn about new practices through several stages. These stages are known as:

i) *The awareness stage*—when a person comes to know of a new practice but lacks the complete information;

ii) *The interest stage*—when he becomes interested in a new idea and wants to know more about it;

iii) *The evaluation stage*—when he mentally applies the new idea to his present situation and evaluates it;

iv) *The trial stage*—when he applies the new idea or practice on a small scale in order to determine its utility under his own situation; and

v) *Adoption stage*—when he decides to continue the full use of the practice.

Thus, it is the cumulative effect on people through exposure to an idea repeatedly that results in action.

REFERENCES

Banoor, D., Harrison, J.Q., *Agricultural Extension—Training and Visit System*, World Bank, Washington, 1977.

Choubay, B.K. *A Handbook of Extension Education*, Jyoti Prakashan, Allahabad, 1979.

Directorate of Extension, *Extension Education in Community Development*, Ministry of Food and Agriculture, Govt. of India, New Delhi. 1961.

Khan P. M. *Textbook of Extension Education*, Himansu Publication, Udaipur, 2002.

Kumar, B.K., Hansra, Extension Education for Human Resource Development. Concept Publishing Company, New Delhi. 2000.

Leagans J.P., "A concept of the Extension Education Process", in *Cooperative Extension Work*, (eds.) L.D. Kelsey and C.C. Hearne. Cornell University Press, Ithaca, New York. 1967.

Ray, G.L. *Extension Communication and Management*, Naya Prokash, Calcutta. 1999.

Reddy, A.A. *Extension Education*, Shree Lakshmi Press, Baptala. AP. 1976.

Van Den Ben A.W., H.S. Hawkins *Agricultural Extension*. Long man Seicntific and Technical Publication. U.S.A. 1994.

5

Agricultural Education in India: Opportunities and Challenges

Agriculture is the mainstay of Indian economy. It provides food to our millions and raw materials for our industries. Our country has enormous potential as an exporter of agricultural commodities. The variety of climatic types and natural conditions offer a conducive environment for the cultivation of a large variety of agricultural produce.

Work in agricultural sectors ranges from the totally academic pursuits of research and teaching to inspection and other supervisory work to commercial activities of establishing farms, plantations, orchards and carrying on exports of produce from them. Agriculture is no longer practised by rule of thumb, instead it has become highly scientific, sophisticated and mechanised and consequently, very profitable too. Horticulture, dairying and poultry farming are allied agricultural activities that have become economically viable opportunities today. The impact of agriculture is not only on the production of food grains, vegetables and fruits, but on so many agriculture dependent industries which get its raw material from agriculture sector. A good monsoon would drive the sensex raging as bull, while floods or other such calamities would bring it to a grinding halt.

Following are major career areas in the field of agriculture:

i) Agricultural research

ii) Agri-business

iii) Agro-industry

iv) Agricultural education

v) Agricultural journalism
vi) Services in agriculture
vii) Banking
vii) Farming
viii) Conservation
ix) Agricultural engineering
x) Management

Basic training in agriculture is offered as a Bachelor's degree course of three to four years duration at all the agricultural universities in the country. The minimum eligibility required for admission to B.Sc.(Ag.) course is a pass in the plus two or equivalent examination with science or agriculture. Many universities fix a minimum aggregate of 50 per cent marks to be obtained in the qualifying examination. Admission to the different universities may be based on merit or performance in an entrance examination. Notifications of the courses at various places appear from January onwards, while the sessions usually start off between July and September.

More than 40 colleges offer the B.Sc.(Ag.) course, as also the M.Sc.(Ag.) course. Specialisations in agriculture include agricultural economics, agricultural chemistry, animal husbandary and dairy, horticulture, farming system management and agricultural marketing management. Also there are around 20 institutions offering BE Agricultural Engineering Courses.

Job Opportunities

Agriculture in India contributes 29.4 per cent of Gross domestic Product (GDP). Agriculture employs about 64 per cent of the work force for different activities. Agriculture graduates are offered jobs in both public as well as private sector. Agro-industries, public and private sector banks, state and central government departments offer job opportunities to agriculture graduates. Agriculture Assistant and Agriculture Field Officers are recruited by different banks to help them disburse loan to farmers and small entrepreneurs. Qualifications to these posts vary from graduate to post graduate. Central and State Agriculture Departments offer posts of Block Agricultural officers, District Agriculture Officers and District Horticultural Officers etc. Seed certification agencies offer post of Certification Assistant and Certification Officers. Agriculture graduates can compete for posts like Block Development Officers (BDOs), Forest reangers and other posts advertised by Public Service Commissions of different states. Research Assistants are hired by research units of ICAR, SAU's and different multi-national companies (MNC's) involved in manufacturing of seed, insecticides, pesticides and fungicides. Agriculture graduates have plenty of opportunities as an agricultural journalist, radio reporter, extension specialist or subject matter specialist. Opportunities also exist in Tea Gardens, call centres and community centres in the villagers.

Vast opportunities are available to those who wish to pursue higher studies and have an aptitude towards research. ICAR recruits Scientific staff conducting an all India level test. Service is known as Agricultural Research Service (ARS). Minimum qualification for Scientific posts is a post graduate degree in concerned subject. However, one should aspire to ARS after acquiring a doctorate degree as promotion is faster than having minimum qualification. Agriculturists with doctorate can apply for professorship in colleges and universities. Acquiring an MBA or PGDM after graduation may help in getting a job in MNC's. It may also help in establishing an agri-business.

Educational Facilities

India has a very strong agricultural education system in the country consisting of one Central Agricultural University, forty-five State Agricultural Universities (SAUs) and four National Institutes of Indian Council of Agricultural Research having the status of Deemed to be University. Among the Deemed Universities, Indian Agricultural Research Institute (IARI) was established a century ago and was given the status of Deemed University in 1958. The other Deemed Universities viz., Indian Veterinary Research Institute (IVRI), Izzatnagar (U.P.), National Dairy Research Institute (NDRI), Karnal and Central Institute of Fisheries Education (CIFE), Mumbai cater to quality education in animal sciences, dairy and fishery sectors respectively. The SAUs are spread over the entire country and cater to HRD in agriculture and allied fields in different agro-climatic regions.

The agricultural universities in India have excellent infrastructural facilities like laboratories, libraries, computer centres and instructional farms. Generally all universities have residential requirements and students are required to stay in hostels. All foreign students are provided accommodation on the campus. Several universities also have furnished hostels for international students. There are limited hostel facilities for married students also. For cultural exchange and understanding, foreign students are encouraged to stay in the same hostels with other Indian students. However, to overcome constraints faced by them particularly with different food habits, Council is in the process of constructing foreign student's hostels in SAU's and DU's. For all round development of students, sports and games facilities on all campuses are available in each Universities/ Institutes.

Department of Agricultural Research And Education

Agricultural education and research in the India is promoted and coordinated by the Department of Agricultural Research And Education (DARE). Admissions of foreign students in various Indian agriculture universities/ ICAR Institutes are also coordinated by the DARE as it acts as a nodal agency for International Cooperation in the area of agricultural research and education in India and provides the necessary government linkages for the Indian Council of Agricultural Research (ICAR). Indian Council of Agricultural Research (ICAR) and Central Agricultural University (CAU), Imphal, are two autonomous bodies under the administrative control of DARE. There are four deemed to be universities (DU's) under the ICAR that awards post graduate degrees in the field of agriculture, dairy, fisheries and veterinary sciences. These deemed to be universities are listed below.

i) Indian Agricultural Research institute, New Delhi

ii) National Dairy Research Institute, Karnal

iii) Indian Veterinary research Institute, Izatnagar

iv) Central Institute on Fisheries Education, Mumbai

With an objective to maintain high quality of education in agriculture, Indian Council of agricultural Research has long back formed "Education Division" at its headquarters in Delhi which is headed by a Deputy Director General (Education). Deputy Director General (Education) is assisted by three Assistant Director Generals (ADGs) responsible for three sections in the division namely, human resource development, education planning/development and educational quality assurance/ reforms. Education division of ICAR achieves its objectives through partnership with State Agricultural Universities (SAUs), Deemed to be Universities, Central Agricultural University and Central Universities with Agriculture faculty.

Indian Institute of Technology, Kharagpur, is the lone IIT that have a separate agriculture department known as Department of Agriculture and food Engineering. This department offers few courses at UG and PG level and also Ph.D. degrees in various agricultural subjects. Several traditional universities have affiliated agricultural colleges that used to impart agricultural education in India before establishment of Agricultural Universities. Colleges in Agra, Baraut, Varanasi and Kanpur were few famous colleges to name in the past.

Education Division of ICAR provides regular financial and professional support to SAUs, CUs and DUs for modernisation and strengthening of academic facilities, infrastructure and faculty improvement. It also has a National Centre for Agricultural Economics and Policy Research and a management academy known as National Academy of Agricultural Research Management (NAARM) at Hyderabad for imparting management training to scientific staff of National Agricultural Research System (NARS) in India. Education Division of ICAR conducts examination for admission in different agricultural universities for quality up-gradation and every year about 1350 (15 per cent of total seats) meritorious candidates are admitted through these tests in UG programmes and 1600 (25 per cent of total seats) in PG programmes.

State Agricultural Universities offer UG courses such as B.Sc (Ag) and AH, B.V. Sc and AH, B. Tech (Agl. Engg.), PG courses in Agronomy, Plant Breeding, Seed Technology, Plant Pathology, Entomology, Soil Science, Soil Microbiology, Soil Chemistry, Agricultural Biotechnology,. Agriculture Extension etc. Students having interest in research may pursue higher studies in these subjects as most of these courses are available in almost all universities. ICAR offers scholarships to meritorious students at all levels of study. Scholarships for pursuing higher studies are offered by other organisations as well. Council of Scientific and Industrial Research also supports post graduate students opting for courses in agriculture.

Central Agricultural University

The Central Agricultural University has been established by an act of Parliament, the Central Agricultural University Act 1992 (No.40 of 1992). The Act came into effect on 26th January, 1993 with the issue of necessary notification by the Department of Agricultural Research and Education (DARE), Govt. of India. The University became functional with the joining of first Vice-Chancellor on 13th September, 1993. The jurisdiction of the University extends to six North-Eastern Hill States viz., Arunachal Pradesh, Manipur, Meghalaya, Mizoram, Sikkim and Tripura, with headquaters at Imphal in Manipur.

The mission of the University is to be a centre of excellence in teaching, research and extension education in the field of agriculture and allied sectors. The University aims to develop sustainable farming systems for improving productivity and profitability in agriculture and allied sectors and also train the farmers and extension functionaries for the effective dissemination of advanced agricultural technologies in North East India.

The University acts as an important link in the chain for converting agriculture and allied vocations into profitable enterprises and offering food and nutritional security for the people of North-East region. To realise the above mission, University established seven colleges and three Krishi Vigyan Kendras (KVKs) in the six states of North-East India and offers Undergraduate and Postgraduate Degree Programmes in agriculture and allied sciences.

Mandates, Mission, Goals and Objectives

Mandates: The objectives and mandates of the university as stipulated in the Act are:

- To impart education in different branches of agriculture and allied science as it may deem fit;
- To further the advancement of learning and conducting of research in agriculture and allied sciences;
- To undertake extension education programme in the states under its jurisdiction; and
- To undertake such other activities, as it may deem fit, from time to time.

Mission: Keeping the mandates view, the mission of the university is to be a center of Excellence in teaching, research and extension education in the field of agriculture and allied sciences.

Goals: To fulfill the mission, the university has set the following goals for itself:

- To produce globally competitive graduates and postgraduates in agriculture and allied sciences;
- To develop sustainable and profitable farming system for improving productivity, production and profitability in the agriculture and allied sectors;
- To educate the extension functionaries for effective dissemination of agro technologies to the farmers, entrepreneurs and agro-industries; and
- To be an important link in the chain for converting agriculture and allied vocations into profitable enterprises and providing food and nutritional security to the people of NE Region, and the world.

Objectives: To meet the goals, the university has laid down the following objectives:

- To establish and develop excellent constituent colleges that offer undergraduate and postgraduate education in various states of the NE region coming under the jurisdiction of the university in the field of agriculture, agricultural engineering, fisheries, home science, horticulture, forestry and veterinary science and animal husbandry;
- To impart quality education so as to produce globally competitive graduates and post-graduates in different areas of agriculture and allied sciences including

interdisciplinary areas, who are confident and capable of working as scientists, entrepreneurs, managers, agro-industrial workers and above all progressive farmers;

- To establish research stations and specialised research laboratories for taking up basic and applied research by the scientists and postgraduate students;
- To develop and demonstrate alternate farming systems which help the farmers to improve their productivity and profitability while preserving and improving the environment;
- To establish transfer of technology centre including Krishi Vigyan Kendras (Farm Science Centres) for developing effective extension methodologies and training the trainers in information dissemination;
- To popularise improved farming systems, technologies and equipment on pilot basis to be model for other extension agencies;
- To offer short-term refresher and vocational courses and training programmes to the officials of state government departments, farmers, entrepreneurs and agro-industrial houses;
- To have collaborations in the field of teaching, research, transfer of technology and developmental activities with the development departments of the states and national and international institutions including industrial and business houses;
- To provide consultancy services to progressive farmers, agro-entrepreneurs, agro- industries and others involved in agriculture and allied sectors; and
- To act as documentation and information centre on agricultural education, research, extension methodology and development.

Major Campuses under CAU

The University is authorised to establish seven major campuses in six states falling under its jurisdiction (Table 1).

Table 1. Major Campuses under CAU

No.	College/Campus	State
1	College of Agriculture, Iroisemba, Imphal	Manipur
2	College of Vety. Sciences and A.H., Aizawl	Mizoram
3	College of Fisheries, Lembucherra, Agartala	Tripura
4	College of Horticulture and Forestry, Pasighat	Arunachal Pradesh
5	College of Home Science, Tura	Meghalaya
6	College of Agricultural Engineering and Post-Harvest Technology	Sikkim
7	College of Post-Graduate Studies, Barapani	Meghalaya

Courses Offered

At present, under-graduate programmes are offered in eleven major disciplines such as Agriculture, Horticulture, Fisheries, Forestry, Home Science, Sericulture, Agricultural Engineering, Dairy Technology, Food Science and Technology, Agricultural Marketing, Banking and Cooperation, and Veterinary Science. At Post-graduate level programmes are offered in as many as 65 different disciplines. All Universities also offer Ph.D. programmes in these subjects.

Table 2. Courses Offered by CAU

Course	Duration	Eligibility Requirements
B.Sc. (Agriculture)	4 Year Programme	10+2 or equivalent in Science/ Agriculture with Physics, Chemistry and Mathematics/Biology/ Agriculture with at least 60 per cent marks or equivalent OGPA.
B.Sc. (Horticulture)	4 Year Programme	10+2 with Physics, Chemistry and Biology with 60 per cent marks equivalent OGPA
B.Sc. (Fisheries)	4 Year Programme	10+2 with Physics, Chemistry and Biology with 60 per cent marks equivalent OGPA
B.Sc. (Forestry)	4 Year Programme	10+2 with Physics, Chemistry and Biology or Mathematics with 60 per cent marks or equivalent OGPA. Physical fitness is also essential.

B.Sc. (Home Science) Hons	4 Year Programme	10+2 with Physics, Chemistry and Biology, Agriculture/Home Science with at least 60 per cent marks or equivalent OPGA.
B.Sc. (Sericulture)	4 Year Programme	10+2 with Physics, Chemistry and Biology or Mathematics with 60 per cent marks or equivalent OGPA
B. Tech.(Agricultural Engineering)	4 Year Programme	10+2 with Physics, Chemistry and Mathematics or equivalent with at least 60 per cent marks or equivalent OPGA.
B. Tech. (Dairy Technology)	4 Year Programme	10+2 with Physics, Chemistry and Mathematics or equivalent with at least 60 per cent marks or equivalent OPGA
B. Tech. (Food Science and Technology)	4 Year Programme	10+2 with Physics, Chemistry and Biology or Mathematics with 60 per cent marks or equivalent OPGA
B.Sc. (Agril. Mktg., Banking and Coop.)	4 Year Programme	10+2 with Physics, Chemistry and Biology or Mathematics with 60 per cent marks or equivalent OPGA
B.V.Sc. and A.H	5 Year Programme	10+2 with Physics, Chemistry and Biology or equivalent with at least 60 per cent marks or equivalent OGPA
M.Sc./M.J./M.Tech./M.V.Sc	2 year Programme	Must have completed their Under-graduation in Agriculture relevant disciplines and secured on OGPA of 7.00 out of 10.00 or 60 per cent marks or equivalent at the graduation level in respective discipline. Those coming with graduation in Science will have to take one year courses in Agriculture for M.Sc.(A.) programmes. For M.V.Sc. programme. The candidates must have completed B.V.Sc. and A.H. programme of 5 years duration and also internship programme of six months duration.

Academics

The Director of instruction is responsible for planning, coordination and supervision of academic programmes of the university in various faculties. As per te mandate, the university has established constituent colleges, one each in the faculties of agriculture, fisheries, home science, horticulture and forestry and veterinary and animal science. A college in the faculty of agricultural Engineering and an inter- disciplinary post graduate college are in the process of being established. The colleges are spread in various states of the NE Region coming under the jurisdiction of the university.

System of Education

The university follows semester system of education with 10 point scale of grading. It has internal-cum-external system of examination and evaluation. The university has adopted model academic regulations and syllabi as proposed by the Indian council of Agricultural Research/ Veterinary council of India with some minor changes to suit the regional needs.

The minimum qualification for admission to undergraduate programmes is a pass in 10+2 in science or equivalent examination with physics, Chemistry and Biology / Mathematics combination, while for postgraduate programmes, the candidates must have obtained a Bachelor's degree in the concerned/ related subjects. Candidates seeking admission should be a permanent resident or domicile of any of the states of the NE Region, covered under the jurisdiction of the university. However, this condition is not applicable to the nominees of ICAR/VCI or any special category of nominees as decided by the university / Department of Agricultural Research and Education, Government of India.

Based on the population of each constituent state, quota has been fixed for undergraduate programmes for various states and the admission is given to the candidates sponsored by the respective states based on the common entrance test conducted by them. In addition to states' quota, 15 per cent seats for undergraduate programmes are filled up by the ICAR/VCI, based on all-India entrance examination.

The postgraduate seats to the extent of 75 per cent are filled by the university based on the merit in qualifying degree, whereas

25 per cent seats are earmarked for ICAR which are filled on the basis of all-India entrance test.

Research

The Director of Research is responsible for supervision and coordination of research programmes in the university. The research activities under CAU aims at developing technologies which can bring about a far reaching impact on productivity and production of crops, animals and fishes through sustainable and eco-friendly technological approaches for the socio-economic development in the region. With these objectives, a number of need-based, location-specific internally-funded research programmes are being carried out under Intramural Research Projects (IRP) and also externally funded research projects in all constituent colleges.

Extension

The Director of Extension Education is responsible for the supervision and coordination of all extension education activities of the university. The university is making sincere efforts to enhance its capacity in the field of teaching, research and extension education so as to effectively fulfill its mandates.

National Academy of Agricultural Research Management

The National Academy of Agricultural Research Management (NAARM) was established by the Indian Council of Agricultural Research (ICAR) at Hyderabad, in 1976, to address issues related to agricultural research and education management. In the initial years, the Academy primarily imparted foundation training to the new entrants of the Agricultural Research Service of ICAR. Subsequently, its role expanded to include research, capacity building of senior professionals of national and international NARS in agricultural research and education management, and policy and consultancy support to NARS.

The Academy also renders services for building IP portfolios like patents and geographical indications to various stakeholders including farmers and scientists. Keeping in view the increasing national and global need to integrate agriculture with agribusiness for raising rural incomes, and the increased emphasis on the creation, dissemination, application and exchange of knowledge in this vital area, the Academy has recently initiated post graduate education programmes and set up an Agribusiness Knowledge Centre

Indian NARS is one of the largest systems in agricultural research in the world employing over 25,000 scientists, who work in institutes distributed throughout the entire length and breadth of the country. Judicious and proper management of this vast manpower poses a formidable challenge to the system. Keeping in view this objective, the Government of India has established the National Academy of Agricultural Research Management (NAARM), Hyderabad.

Since its inception in 1976, the Academy has expanded its horizon of activities over the years. Through its innovative training and research programmes in the specialised areas of Agricultural Research and Education Management, it has helped the systems in evolving appropriate policies to improve the efficiency and effectiveness of research and education in particular and agriculture at large. Its scope has been further widened to encompass tailor-made training, especially for the international participants from the developing countries in Asia, Africa and Latin America. Research on management problems has formed another major activity of the Academy. This has provided an input for improvising training and the policy support.

The Academy extends a facilitative role to the ICAR in developing policy guidelines on the various issues related to personnel, Organisation and Management reforms, human resource development, assessment system, and others, all of which are aimed at improving the overall efficiency and effectiveness of the NARS. NAARM has been developing itself into a resource centre for management needs. On the strength of the experienced and expert faculty, the Academy has started offering specialised consultancy services in the areas of its mandated activities.

The Academy strives to generate a sense of fraternity and inculcate a scientific work culture amongst the agricultural scientists and teachers in the country. Being a unique institution of its kind, the Academy is well poised to augment its usefulness and aims to emerge as an institution par excellence to facilitate and support a culture of dynamic management in agricultural research and education.

Objectives

The Academy id committed to promote professionalism in the management of agricultural education, research and extension programmes and agri-business, and enhance the efficiency, responsiveness, and performance of the National Agricultural System (NAS). It aims:

i) To impart agricultural management education;

i) To enhance the teaching-learning effectiveness through proper management of agricultural education;

i) To plan and organise need-based, multi-tier, stakeholder-driven and customised on-campus and off-campus training programmes;

i) To facilitate knowledge and technology dissemination management through innovative use of Information and Communication Technologies (ICTs);

i) To undertake research on agricultural and technology management, and address emerging concerns in agriculture;

i) To offer consultancy and manage dialogues to backstop training and to provide policy support to NAS;

i) To develop suitable management tools, practices and processes for facilitating organisational effectiveness;

i) To assemble quality resource material and function as a resource centre of information and knowledge;

i) To promote facilitative work culture for fostering creativity and innovativeness;

i) To enhance administrative and financial management in the system;

i) To forge and strengthen partnerships, linkages and networking at regional, national and global levels; and

i) To take up other related activities for fulfilling the mandate.

By the year 2025, the Academy will emerge as India's premier Institute of Excellence in the field of Agricultural Management, known and sought nationally and globally for its expertise in management of agricultural education, research, training, consultancy, public policy programmes and agri-business, and will contribute significantly to promote the sustainable growth and development of agriculture

Organisation

The Academy receives guidance for its effective functioning from the Institute Management Committee (IMC) and Research Advisory Committee (RAC), comprising the Directors and eminent scientists from within and outside the Academy. There are also Academic and Research Councils, to guide the training and research activities of the Academy. To effectively implement its mandated activities, the Academy is organised under three Divisions, supported by various centralised services.

Krishi Vigyan Kendras

The Second Education Commission (1964-66) under the chairmanship of Dr. D. S. Kothari, recommended for the establishment of agricultural polytechnics to provide vocational education in agriculture to school dropouts and other rural youths. After careful deliberation by the Ministry of Education, Ministry of Agriculture and the Planning Commission and as a follow up of the recommendation, the Indian Council of Agricultural Research (ICAR) appointed a committee under the Chairmanship of Dr. Mohan Singh Mehta of Seva Mandir, Udaypur in 1973 for formulating the institutional design of Krishi Vigyan Kendras (KVK) for providing vocational training in agriculture.

The basic principles enunciated by the Mehta Committee (1973) include:

- The Kendra will impart learning through work-experience and hence will be concerned with technical literacy, the acquisition of which does not necessarily require the ability to read and write.
- The Kendra will impart training only to those extension workers who are employed and to the practising farmers

and fishermen. In other words, the Kendra will cater to the needs of those who are already employed or those who wish to be self-employed.

– There will be no uniform syllabus for the Kendras. The syllabus and programme of each Kendra will be flexible in nature and tailored according to the felt needs, natural resources and potential for agricultural growth in that particular area.

Krishi Vigyan Kendras (Farm Science Centre), an innovative science based institutions, were thus established mainly to impart vocational training to the farmers and field level extension workers. The concept of vocational training in agriculture through KVK grew substantially due to greater demand for improved agricultural technology by the farmers. They not only required knowledge and understanding of the intricacy of technologies, but also progressively more and more skills in various complex agricultural operations for adoption on their farms. The effectiveness of the KVK was further enhanced by adding the activities related to on-farm testing and Front-Line Demonstration on major agricultural technologies in order to make the training of farmers location specific, need based and resource-oriented.

The training programmes were designed to impart the latest knowledge to the farmers through work experience by applying the principles of 'Teaching by Doing' and 'Learning by Doing'. The prime goal of KVK is to impart training as per needs and requirements in agriculture and allied enterprises to all farmers, farm women and farm youths including school drop-outs in the rural area.

No formal certificate or diploma is awarded, irrespective of duration of the courses to avoid the rush for jobs instead of self employment. While designing the courses, the concept of farming system as well as farming situation are taken into account to ensure that the enterprises in which they are trained are commercially and ecologically viable, sustainable and profitable. Such vocational trainings help them to sustain themselves through self-employment and to make them self-reliant economically and thus discourages them to migrate to the urban areas.

KVKs provide training not only in agriculture and allied vocations but also in other income-generating activities that may supplement the income of farm families. The methods employed in training could be formal and non-formal or a combination of both, depending upon the needs but emphasis remains to be on work-experience, as suggested by Mohan Singh Mehta Committee Report that "the programme should be operated as a plan of continuing education both in the technical and general sense

Objectives

The KVKs are light houses of knowledge to the farming community of India. Its' main objectives are:

- Planning and conducting survey of the operational area in order to prepare the resource inventory with special reference to identifying the training needs of the farming community.
- Planning and conducting production- oriented, need-based short and long duration training courses both on campus as well as in the villages for various target groups with priority on the weaker and the poor.
- Developing and organising non-formal educational programmes by way of field days, farm visits, farmers fair, radio talk, Farm Science clubs etc. as the follow up information support to training courses.
- Organising farm science clubs, both in rural schools and in villages in order to induce in younger generation a liking for and an interest for agricultural and allied sciences and scientific farming through supervised projects.
- Developing and maintaining the campus farms and demonstration units on scientific lines as the facilities for providing work experience to the trainees as also disseminating the latest technical know how.
- Providing practical facilities of the Kendra to the teachers and the students of the vocational agriculture of the higher secondary schools.
- Imparting some general education to rural illiterates and school drop-outs in order to make them not only good farmers but also better citizens.

- Providing added training facilities in the areas for home making and nutrition education for rural community.
- Gradually enlarging the training facilities to encompass other important areas such as home crafts , cottage industries etc. consistent to the requirements of the Integrated rural Development in collaboration with concerned organisation.
- Implementing all such schemes of the ICAR and other related organisations which intend to strengthen the training programmes of the Kendra.

Mandates of KVKs

The first KVK, on a pilot basis, was established in 1974 at Pondicherry under the administrative control of Tamil Nadu Agricultural University, Coimbatore. The mandates of KVKs are as follows-

- Conducting "on-farm testing" for identifying technologies in terms of location specific sustainable land use systems.
- Organising training to update the extension personnel with emerging advances in agricultural research on regular basis.
- Organising short and long term training courses in agriculture and allied vocations for the farmers and rural youths with emphasis on "Learning by doing" for higher production on farms and generating self-employment.
- Organising Front Line Demonstrations (FLDs) on various crops to generate production data and feed back information.

In order to achieve the above mandates, the following broad objectives would help the KVKs to develop their specific objectives:

- To promptly demonstrate the latest agricultural technologies to the farmers as well as extension workers of State Departments of Agriculture/Horticulture/ Fishery/ Animal Science/ NGOs with a view to reduce the time lag between the technology generation and its adoption.

- To test and verify the technologies in the socio-economic conditions of the farmers with a view to study the production constraints and to modify the technologies to make them appropriate.
- To impart trainings to the practising farmers/ farm women, rural youth and field level extension functionaries by following the methods of "Teaching by doing" and "Learning by doing'.
- To back-up with training and communication supports to the district level development departments viz; Agriculture/ Horticulture/ Fisheries/ Animal science and NGOs in their extension programmes.

Advisory Committee

All the KVKs have constituted the Scientific Advisory Committee as per the guidelines of ICAR which comprises of representatives from ICAR institutes, State Agriculture University, Development departments of the District, Media personnel, Financial institutions and progressive farmers and farm women. Apart from the members special invitees also attend the meeting. On an average 16 members and 4 invitees attend each Scientific Advisory Committee meeting of KVK. The Scientific Advisory Committee meetings are conducted to get necessary guidance and support to carry out the mandated activities of KVK in a more planned and scientific manner.

KVK Training

The KVKs, thus are the down-to-earth institutions committed to vocational training, transfer of latest technologies, on farm research and thus, serving as the light house for overall rural development in the district. The activities of the KVK include technology assessment, refinement and transfer, aiming to bridge the gap between the technology developed at the research institutions and its adoption at the field level by the farmers through demonstration of technology/ products etc. and training of farmers, rural youths and extension personnel. On the basis of "India-2002", there were 578 rural districts spread over the country and this figure has further been raised to 602 districts as per the latest data available on the internet report of NIC.

Table 3. Number of Krishi Vigyan Kendras

Krishi Vigyan Kendras	No.of KVKs
Zone I – 62 KVKs	
Delhi	1
Haryana	18
Himachal Pradesh	12
Jammu and Kashmir	14
Punjab	17
Zone II – 77 KVKs	
A & N Islands	1
Bihar	38
Jharkhand	21
West Bengal	17
Zone III – 70 KVKs	
Assam	20
Arunachal Pradesh	12
Manipur	9
Meghalaya	5
Mizoram	8
Nagaland	8
Sikkim	4
Tripura	4
Zone IV – 79 KVKs	
Uttar Pradesh	66
Uttaranchal	13
Zone V – 55 KVKs	
Andhra Pradesh	22
Maharashtra	33
Zone VI - 57 KVKs	
Rajasthan	32
Gujarat	25
Zone VII – 93 KVKs	
Chattisgarh	16
Madhya Pradesh	47
Orissa	30
Zone VII – 76 KVKs	
Karnataka	27
Tamil Nadu	30
Kerala	14
Goa	2
Pondicherry	2
Lakshadweep	1

In view of continuous increase in the number of districts, it is agreed to have one KVK in each district by the end of Xth plan. Realising the importance of technology assessment, refinement and transfer, the Planning Commission has allocated Rs. 500 crores specifically for the establishment of new KVKs during Xth plan period. The DDG(AE) during the 11th EFC meeting of Xth plan, held in New Delhi on 30th Sept. 2003 out lined the importance of two issues in the context of the present scenario of agriculture in India: (a) the technologies have to be assessed and refined before their transfer and (b) a programme approach involving various technology components relevant to the farmers in varying farming situations will be required for a perceptible change. The concept of technology assessment and refinement is based on participatory mode ensuring greater scientists-farmer linkage and access to agricultural technologies generated by research systems to the farming community. For this, the role of KVKs are of immense importance for overall agricultural and rural development through its various research and technology transfer mechanisms.

Distance Agricultural Education Programmes

With ever increasing demand for higher education in agriculture and allied subjects in India, the conventional SAUs and other schools were left with inadequate resources for meeting the demand. Thus the distance education system shouldered the responsibility of agricultural education to some extent.

A few open universities are offering education programmes related to agriculture leading to various degrees. The Yashwantrao Chavan Maharashtra Open University (YCMOU) Nashik, Maharashtra, India is pioneer in distance agricultural education programmes.

Agricultural Education Programme of YCMOU are given below:

i) *Certificate Course in Gardening*:
   a) Principles and Practices of Gardening
   b) Fruits, Vegetables and Flower Cultivation
   c) Nursery Management
   d) Landscape Gardening

ii) *Foundation in Agricultural Sciences*:

a) Principles and Practices in Soil Science
b) Principles and Practices in Plant Sciences
c) Principles and Practices in Plant Protection
d) Principles and Practices in Crop Production

iii) *Diploma in Fruit Production:*

a) Principles and Practices of Fruit Production
b) Commercial Fruit Production Part-I
c) Commercial Fruit Production part-II
d) Post Harvest Technology of Fruits

iv) *Diploma in Vegetable Production:*

a) Principles and Practices of Vegetable Production
b) Commercial Vegetable Production Part-I
c) Commercial Vegetable Production Part-II
d) Post Harvest Technology of Vegetables

v) *Diploma in Floriculture and Landscape Gardening:*

a) Principles and Practices of Floriculture
b) Commercial Flower Production Part-I
c) Commercial Flower Production Part-II
d) Post Harvest Technology of Flower and Landscaping

vi) *Diploma in Agri-business Management*:

a) Principles and Practices of Agribusiness Management
b) Agri business Management Part-I
c) Agri business Management Part-II
d) Principles and Practices of Agri business Communication.

vii) *Bachelor of Science in Agriculture and Horticulture (B.Sc. Agri. and B.Sc. Hort.):*

For this 20 courses each are offered and the students have to pass entrance test and submit project report to qualify for the degree.

viii) *Master of Science in Agricultural Communication, Agricultural Extension and Agricultural Development*:

a) Principle and Practices in Distance Education
b) Research Methods and Statistical Analysis
c) Agricultural Extension and Farm Journalism
d) Agricultural Communication and Mass Media
e) Dissertation / Thesis

ix) *Ph.D. in Agricultural Communication / Agriculture Extension/ Agriculture Development:*

a) Principle and Practices of Distance Education
b) Research Methods and Statistical Analysis
c) Agricultural Development and Multimedia Communication
d) Agricultural Information Technology
e) Dissertation/Thesis

The Indira Gandahi National Open University (IGNOU), Delhi offers only one course i.e. B.Tech. Agril. Engineering and all other OUs have yet to start Agricultural Education.

Agriculture is an applied science and hence development in cognitive, psychomotor and affective domain is necessary to achieve quality and effectiveness in people, products and profits through agriculture per se. The effectiveness of distance agricultural education with limited assess to field work and laboratory work and dependency on study centres for such facilities needs serious thinking. Large infrastructure, research and experimental farms with Conventional Agricultural Universities and Schools for the quality output is being strengthened. The DE can support the conventional systems in this regard.

Quality of Distance Education Programmes

Undoubtedly a creation cost effective, high accessibility educational system for accommodating the educationally deprived youth is eminent. The conventional Agricultural Schools of National, Regional and State level could accommodate only about 2 per cent youth who desire to opt for agricultural education. Hence Distance Education through Open Universities is option of prospects. Undoubtedly it should not be at the cost of quality of education and training. It is said that best teaching

/ learning situation is that which is easy to access and use. Open Universities provide this education at low cost. Putting more students in a class or huge registration may lower the cost of education but quality goes down. Distance Agricultural Education quality-wise has inherent limitations about field practicals and laboratory experimentation and interactive learning. Care has to be taken that distance education does not become convenience education at the cost of quality. Limitations and preoccupations of the identified study centres also affect their involvement in the instructional programmes of OU students. Hence target orientedness must be at backseat.

In particular, the students admitted for higher education leading to Ph.D. in Agricultural Communication, Agricultural Extension and Agricultural Development must possess adequate basic knowledge and qualification. It is seen that students with post graduation in Agricultural Engineering, Agricultural Botany or for that matter any other subject are registered for Ph.D. programme in Communication and Agril. Extension. In fact for Ph.D. in these subjects needs in-depth knowledge of research methodology in communication and social sciences. At times, their "Research Guides" are also not from the discipline of communication and / or Extension Education. Under such cases the authenticity and fidelity of the Ph.D. degree may be at stake.

Open Universities are a striking example of independent and interactive learning. They operate at scale and take full advantage of their large scale to produce high quality material at relatively low cost. For interactive activities they engage on contract large number of tutors and research guides to be in direct contact with students. These tutors and research guides are expected to be experts in their subjects and be able to give high quality support to students. These Universities or for that matter distance education per se should not be just a tool for distribution of various degrees / diploma and certificates. Hence, it is essential to recognise the learning and teaching disabilities of the concerned human resource being involved in the distance education process leading to agricultural education.

Educational Expenditure

Expenditure on education of the total budgeted expenditure on education in First Five Year Plan was 9 per cent, in 4th Plan 25 per cent, 5th 22 per cent and came down to 10 per cent in 10th plan. It indicates that government has reduced the funding for higher education. Expenditure of OUs is very low and funds mainly come through student fees. It is seen that funds for student support services, library facilities, instructional material, multimedia production and design and development of course material are low.

Although the major focus of 10th Plan is to raise enrolment of population between age 18 to 23 years from 6 per cent to 10 per cent, the funding for the OUs is provided on net deficit basis. It adversely affects the quality of education. Undoubtedly increasing enrolment is not the wise remedy for this. Government support needs to be increased.

Instructional Methods

Distance Education in agriculture characterised by relatively less interactive teaching / learning programmes. The instructional programmes are mainly dominated by Printed Literature, Postal Correspondence, multimedia technologies and cyber technology. Subject matter and instructional programmes are mainly IT based. Obviously, the hand on experience is extremely less. Extensive use and development of programmed printed lessons, programmed audio and video lessons and programme computer aided instructional material is therefore eminent. Country-wide classroom of UGC and IGNOU on national TV network has become very effective over last several years. But the time slot is very inadequate and devoid of prime time opportunities. In fact for distance education full time TV channel with 24 hour telecast is necessary. A large network of tele-conferencing and internet networking facilities for learners at cooperative / study centres is necessary. Distance education has to become techno-based and cyber based to cater to large information needs fastly.

Distance education is very effective, accessible, low cost educational opportunity for those, out of conventional educational system. However, to be effective in agriculture more practical field based approach is needed. Higher education leading to Ph.D. needs to be more responsibly managed. There are several micro and macro issues before distance education system in general and agriculture in particular in India. Dependence on conventional system, lack of need based training to faculty, service guarantee for academics lacking, lack of adequate and qualified human resources, inadequate funds, doubts about quality of instructional programmes, poor incentives to hired faculty, poor interaction with students and quality of guidance and high dropout rate. Hence to overcome these disabilities and strengthen distance education system in India, it is necessary to strengthen dual mode of distance education and increase government funding in future.

Challenges in Agricultural Education

Agricultural education have been geared to harness the modern science and technology for higher productivity and production. This substantially helped to reduce the food scarcity in India. But sustainable food production is still the primary pursuit. Economic liberalisation and international trade policies pose a big challenge to Indian agriculture. To cope up with changed global scenario, agricultural education and extension would have to be redefined. This is a major concern for academics and policy makers.

Agricultural education has to identify its role in equipping the human resources for enhanced agricultural productivity and sustainable use of natural resources. Agricultural colleges and universities were initially assigned to disseminating scientific knowledge and skills to the farming community and to train them to use such skills for better output. As a backup for such a mission, agricultural research was encouraged to adapt the scientific knowledge to suit to the realities of rural societies. However, these initiatives could not keep pace with the fast changing scientific and technical improvements and gradually failed in their objective to cultivate the most modern skills and attitudes to both agricultural students and farmers. Developing a mechanism to update the curricula of agricultural education and extension, at least on a five-year regular basis, is crucial. This is very relevant to teaching, research and extension functions of the university as they form the inter-related, theoretical and practical basis of modern agricultural education in India.

Economic liberalisation and GATT negotiations demand manifold re-orientations in our agricultural education and extension system. Market oriented agricultural education and extension along with changes in agricultural marketing policy for the national and international markets is the need of the hour. A cadre of social scientists with clear insight into agricultural related disciplines, such as agricultural economics, agri-business, marketing management, rural sociology, agricultural anthropology, agricultural ethics and politics, has to be built up to provide the back up for solving the problem of globalisation in agriculture. This will imply total re-organisation of agricultural education with emphasis on other agricultural related social sciences and effective agricultural policy research. Such a re-organisation will empower our agri-graduates and scientists to face up the challenges posed by the demand of the national and international markets.

Any individual initiative needs certain motivation for sustenance. Pursuing agriculture as a profession / job for a considerable time is also influenced by motivational aspects such as monetary gains, employment, better quality of life and social acceptance. The number of agricultural producers is declining. The population that makes a living directly from agriculture continues to fall in developing countries. People, with rural background and engaged in traditional agriculture, are reluctant to let their children and younger generation to pursue agriculture as a full time profession. Those, with rural background and genuine interest in agriculture, do not have the basic education to go in for higher education in agriculture. This prompted the rural youth to go in for non-agricultural courses and moving in of urban based agriculture graduates without any practical knowledge of agriculture.

Agricultural education has to be made more practical and rural realities oriented while agricultural extensions courses should be tuned to serve the needs of the rural community through dynamic interaction with rural societies. Such extension activities would enrich the academic institutions and universities. Developing countries lag behind in introducing educational courses on environmental and sustainable agriculture. In India, too, there is a need to provide such a curricula re-orientation to academic institutions to create an environment sensitive faculty and to help bring about attitudinal changes among rural communities.

Addressing the Challenges

There has been a dilution in the quality of agricultural education. Agricultural universities, with inadequate infrastructure, financial support and autonomy have mushroomed. To ensure academic excellence, agricultural universities should have complete autonomy coupled with accountability.Dilution in the quality has been, mainly, due to an imbalance in the academic staff structure of the universities. The recruitment policy, and also the policy of freezing new recruitment, needs to be reviewed as presently about 40 per cent of posts are lying vacant in these institutions.

Centralised planning of Agricultural education system and curricula is not addressing the local needs to the extent required. There is tremendous disparity in regional assessment, as quite a number of regions of our country have not been benefited by the developments. There is a need for establishing more Central Agricultural Universities like IIT's.

Rural students need to be encouraged to study in agricultural universities. Steps may be taken to promote such admissions as urban-based agricultural graduates are not so comfortable in rural environment. Specialised courses in educational technology should be developed to upgrade the teaching skills. A Teachers Training Institute in agriculture at the national level would help.

After Research, Teaching and Extension, Training should be the fourth function of the Agricultural Universities. Directorate of HRD and Entrepreneurship could be considered to steer this function.

ICAR and VCI systems of examination and evaluation in the same Agricultural University create disparity in assessing the quality of manpower generated. ICAR and the agricultural education system need an independent regulatory body like the UGC to streamline and give direction to the system.

The agricultural education system needs to be redefined so as to equip the new graduates with subject competency, self motivation, positive attitude, agri-business skills, knowledge of computer and information technology, and communication skills in both English and regional languages.

SAUs should have unified administration and complementarity of departments and multidisciplinary teamwork in the development of programmes of education, research and extension. The Model Act of the ICAR should reflect in the functioning of the State Agricultural Universities (SAUs) and deemed universities. Systems could be put in place at SAUs for quick communication of new knowledge to students in classrooms, extension workers and farmers. SAUs could have flexible course-credit system buttressed by continuous internal evaluation. SAUs could provide regular specialised training to rural youth, particularly school dropouts, and adults who are not eligible for enrolling for formal agricultural courses. An SAU could have corporate board of management with adequate powers under the university act and have organisational and operational autonomy.

The successful models in agriculture demonstrated by the private sector, business groups and industries involved in agriculture should be studied and adopted. The private sector should be given a bigger role in agriculture extension policies/ activities being planned / implemented by the State and Central Governments.

In the liberalised educational policy scenario at the national, regional and global levels, it is essential to have a better coordination between institutions and universities to implement restructured and relevant courses. Private-public partnership, to strengthen the present system of education, research and extension in India, is need of the hour. Roping in talented scientists of the private agri-research sector as guest teachers in Agricultural Universities could be a first step towards this end.

The curriculum should be regularly updated to incorporate the changes in agricultural scenario. Specific curricula could be developed for technological and skill development of women in market driven technological enterprises and sustainable management of natural resources.

The Planning Commission found in 2000 that the contribution of the primary sector (mostly driven by agriculture) was on the decline while the tertiary sector (driven by industry) was having a slower growth. The agricultural education system needs to be reoriented to cater to the needs of the emerging sectors and to ensure that excess manpower is not generated in slow growing sectors.

Agricultural education should lay increased emphasis in future on topics like, alternate farming, bio-fertilizers, pressurised irrigation, integrated water management, integrated nutrient management, integrated pest, disease and weed management, resource optimisation, post harvest technology and value addition, and marketing.

Strategies to Meet the Challenges

The basic objective in redefining agricultural education in the changing scenario is to promote development and delivery of educational programmes that would enhance the employment potential and build up an easy, accessible and cost effective knowledge intensive information system. The guiding principles, approach and strategies are as follows:

i) *Guiding principles*:
   a) Initiatives should have long term impact.
   b) The focus should be on ameliorating quality, relevance and reach.
   c) Linkage with the market requirements and demand of stakeholders.

ii) *Approach*:
   a) Performance and output oriented.
   b) Optimal utilisation of existing infrastructure and resource.

iii) *Strategies*:
   — *Education:*

   Shaping up academic environment through total quality management at all levels.

   Entrepreneurship development and self-employment orientation in agricultural education should receive high priority through infusion of vocational courses (certificate/diploma levels).

   Periodic review and revision of curriculum consistent with national and global scenario, market trends, self-employment avenues and industries requirements.

Make agricultural education an independent subject at school level and integrate it with the higher education system.

Emphasis on distance education in agriculture with extensive use of innovations of IT, digitalisation of course content, virtual universities, e-learning and video conferencing.

Distinguish agricultural education from training for public service, thereby, fostering training aimed at meeting the needs of the private sector and preparing students for entrepreneurship.

Facilitate, promote and support agreements, cooperation and coordination at inter-institutional and international levels.

Promote integration of population, environment and sustainable development themes into agricultural education and extension programme. Include specialised training in degree programmes.

Develop well trained human resource for doing research in advanced areas of science to become internationally competitive.

— *Research:*

Need a paradigm shift from single discipline orientation to multi-disciplinary approach.

Encourage privatisation, planning, monitoring, evaluation and assessment as core component of research management process.

— *Extension:*

Harness benefits of new scientific advances such as biotechnology, cloning, remote sensing, modelling, information and IT for farmers and rural communities. Internet aided extension networks have to be materialised.

KVK's have to be strengthened as nerve centre for dissemination of technical know-how.

Extension programmes to be based on rural participatory approach.

Formation of commodity specific extension kiosk on indigenous food, horticultural crops, livestock, poultry, rabbitry, bee keeping, mushroom, medicinal and aromatic plants, sericulture, tea and value addition enterprises.

Distance education for farmers and small agri-entrepreneurs need to be explored and strengthened through television, radio, interactive audio and video systems, besides print and programmed learning materials which would be the distinguishing feature of extension teaching and learning process.

– Institutional Reforms

Effective partnership linkages with advanced centres of education in the country and abroad.

Greater autonomy to academic institutions, SAUs and statutory power to ICAR.

Ensuring Quality Education

Though quality is a very important issue in Agricultural Education and Extension, it was given least importance at present. A Total Quality Management (TQM) system should be evolved to ensure quality education.

The concept of total quality management must refer to conforming to the expectation of the stakeholders. The paradigm shift in agricultural education should include teaching students not just what is currently known but also to keep them abreast of the new knowledge essential for meeting the challenges of new economic environment and all that would contribute to socio-economic development and public good. The education should lead to development of analytical skills, exposure to international marketing, total quality standards and comparative advantages. It should also facilitate confidence in ensuring sustainability with high productivity and quality of the produce while meeting international standards. Post-harvest technology and value-addition are also key to maximum benefits from exports.

Total quality management in agricultural education needs to focus on improving quality of courses, instructional processes, human centered development, students support services, building strong work culture and electronic communication system. Ultimately, the quality and skills being imparted must inculcate expectations of different stakeholders.

Universities could provide non-formal education and vocational course including technological empowerment of women and rural youth through distance education.

The private colleges that provide high quality agricultural education should be given accreditation with the Central and State Government Universities. These colleges/universities should also be given assistance to sustain their quality and standard.

Training is an important component. Training Institutes of high quality should be established on urgent basis to provide better training to both in-service and out side personnel in agriculture. Distance learning methods are recommended to meet the high demand on training. Exchanging academics between ICAR and SAUs should be encouraged to avoid inbreeding and encourage quality of agricultural education.

Agriculture is increasingly demanding interface with industry, and hence short-term and long-term self-supporting courses on agri-business and marketing should be developed by the Central and State Universities. The experience of IGNOU, and State Open Universities should be taken into account in this regard.

Agricultural students and practitioners are aware of the quality aspects, but they don't put them in practice. This attitude must change. Research, training and extension agriculture should be in continuum in for achieving quality ideals. Young people should be encouraged to the system and contribute fresh ideas.

Practical aspects that need prominence in the curriculum are absent in the present system. SAUs should run short-term courses for Plus-Two level students to enable them in engaging themselves in income generating activities. Suitable tie-ups with industry should also be encouraged to enhance the relevance in agricultural education.

The recommended 10 per cent raise in funding every year is not implemented by the Government and Universities. This adversely affected upgrading the facilities/quality of agricultural education. Centres of Excellencies should be identified and the responsibility of revamping agricultural programmes should be given to these institutions.

Need of Change in Agricultural Education

India's transformation from a country which was a net importer of foodgrains in the early sixties, to one which became an occasional exporter in the eighties is attributed directly, among other factors, to investments in building a large infrastructure by way of agricultural research and educational institutions under the Indian Council of Agricultural Research and under the State-owned Agricultural Universities starting in the early sixties. While India's agricultural research and education system can rightly be credited with ushering in the green revolution of the seventies and eighties, the writing on the wall now is also clear and loud—unless the system now transforms itself in ways which will enable it to face the emerging challenges, the woes of Indian agriculture, already showing up in the form of repeated imports of commodities like wheat and pulses, are bound to increase.

The context of Indian agriculture and its goals is changing and so are the challenges before the research and education system. In the fifties and sixties, the years immediately after independence, the main forcing paradigm for agricultural development was the need and urgency of achieving self-sufficiency in the production of foodgrains in the shortest possible time, to obviate the need of imports in years of calamities and in the context of the growing population. To achieve these development objectives the key strategy adopted by the emerging network of research institutions was to initially focus on the spread of area under high-yielding varieties of selected crops like rice, wheat and maize, and to enhance crop productivity through improved management and use of inputs, including spread of irrigation, fertilizers, crop protection measures, etc., in the relatively well-endowed regions—regions where irrigation facilities were available or could be created easily.

Over the successive five-year plans, the research and education system has expanded to widen the research focus to include an array of field and horticultural crops, livestock species and fisheries. The concept of State Agricultural Universities has also been evolving to emphasise greater focus on livestock health and production, horticultural crops, etc. Past achievements and expanded research and education infrastructure not withstanding, there are clear and increasing evidences that Indian agriculture is tending to stagnate, productivity growth has slowed and this is a cause of serious worry for the country's planners. The average annual growth of the Indian economy in the 10th Plan period estimated at 7 per cent, is poised to further pick up in the coming years. As against this, the annual growth rate from agricultural GDP is unlikely to exceed 1.5 per cent. Even conservative estimates of domestic demand show that growth in annual demand in respect of most agricultural commodities is now outstripping growth in domestic supply, necessitating recurrent dependence on import of foodgrains, pulses, etc. to meet the basic food needs of the still growing population. There appears a general consensus that if India is to move into and sustain double-digit overall economic growth in the coming years, agriculture must aim to grow at a higher trajectory of 4 per cent annual growth. This is then the challenge.

One thing which should be clear at the outset is that the strategies we adopted to enhance agricultural productivity in the past are no longer working. It should also be clear that the nature and dimensions of the challenges we now face are different from what we faced in the sixties and seventies, and for this reason past strategies are unlikely to work—what we now need are strategies and approaches which take into account the nature and dimensions of the new challenges.

The emergence of a new set of challenges can be attributed to a number of factors which obviously include our past agricultural development strategies, current growth patterns and needs, increasing globalisation, and new scientific and technological developments worldwide, etc. In the past, our research strategies were largely focused on enhancing productivity for crops in relatively well-endowed irrigated areas. This must change. Productivity growth emphasis must now focus on a greater variety of crops, farming situations and regions as also on other sectors, including livestock, fisheries, horticultural crops and agro-forestry to address issues of equity and livelihood.

By far the most serious challenge before Indian agriculture is to define and pursue strategies that contribute to the reversal of processes which have caused widespread degradation of natural resources—land, water, biodiversity, following past development strategies. Maintaining and enhancing the quality of resource base is fundamental to improving and sustaining productivity. In the intensively cultivated high-productivity northwest region comprising the states of Punjab, Haryana and western Uttar Pradesh, declining water resource has emerged as the key issue affecting sustainability of agriculture in the region. Declining soil quality and pollution of surface and groundwater resources causing widespread human and livestock health problems due to inappropriate agricultural practices call for a paradigm shift in the ways that agricultural interventions are generated and promoted. In vast areas under rainfed agriculture, issues of resources conservation are a prerequisite to achieving enhanced productivity. Continuing degradation through soil erosion and high run-off rates is adversely impacting resource productivity and in turn the livelihood opportunities of people who depend on these. Issues of biodiversity loss, which form the very basis of sustainable agriculture, have not even been flagged as part of any strategy to address sustainability issues in agriculture. This only spells the seriousness of the future of agriculture.

The key challenge before us is to conceive and promote strategies that integrate the concerns of enhancing productivity and resource conservation and sustainable use. These challenges call for new ways of planning, prioritising and executing our science agenda. A shift to sustainability paradigm calls for a different way of approaching and solving the problems. There are also other challenges before the scientific community. With increased productivity and production being the sole objective of agricultural research, the scientific community emerged as the 'givers' and farmers the 'recipients' of technologies developed through research. The technologies were supposed to have been well 'tested' and refined before these were offered for 'transfer' to farmers, so that farmers could adopt new practices with little risk. In this linear process of technology generation and transfer, farmers became mere 'recipients' of prescription—the process taking little account of farmers' perceptions, knowledge and experience of the environment in which they work, their capacity to innovate and their immediate needs. While this process was inevitable when increased inputs-use was the key to increased productivity in relatively uniform and well-endowed regions, our future efforts to enhance agriculture would demand a shift in mind-set, which recognises the need to view farmers as partners rather than mere recipients of technology.

Change in mindset always takes time, but this is the challenge. There are other aspects also in which the scientific community has to change. While advances in individual scientific disciplines will continue to drive future agricultural changes, solving problems facing the farmers often calls for teams of scientists from different disciplines and organisations to work together—and in this we are not good. The way we are organised in science often promotes individual efforts rather than team efforts aimed at finding solutions to the problems. This is a big challenge to live up to. India's agricultural research system must articulate a structured response to new developments taking place locally, nationally and globally.

A large number of voluntary non-government organisations are working actively with local communities to improve their livelihoods. Similarly, many public-sector undertakings, including banks and private business houses are increasingly investing in activities aimed at helping farming community's access to technologies, advisories, etc. How does the system view these developments vis-a-vis its own agenda? Several private players are already making huge investments in research, particularly in meeting the demands for better quality seeds, planting materials, etc.

In the light of intellectual property right implications, these developments call for the research system to redefine its priorities and strategies. There are other developments taking place nationally and internationally, which have serious implications on the ways that the national system must respond. We now have a separate department for biotechnology and one for earth sciences under the Ministry of Science and Technology. A department for land resource under the Ministry of Rural Development will have a major responsibility in evolving strategies for sustainable land use and management. With agriculture continuing to be a primary land user, a strong interaction would be required to evolve future land-use policies. So will be the case with the departments of environment, water resources, etc.

Consultative Group on International Agricultural Research is moving towards the emergence of a global agricultural research system, with the major aim of contributing global public goods. Regional groupings like APARI (Asia-Pacific Agricultural Research Institutions) are aiming to focus on regional issues. India, with a large national agricultural research system, will need to be increasingly proactive in not only defining its own role, but also in contributing to define the rules of the game in which it wishes to be a significant player. Global developments also call for responses at the global level. Being a part of the global family, India is signatory to several international treaties and conventions, which oblige us to take such steps and actions that will help us protect our resources, while enabling their sustainable use and management.

Being a major land user, these developments have a direct relevance to India's agricultural research system. Crop and plant biodiversity has direct relevance to sustainability of agriculture and food security. Climate change and increased weather variability are already of serious concern in Indian agriculture. At the same time the way in which we develop and promote agricultural practices has a direct effect on greenhouse gas emissions, carbon sequestration, resource degradation, sustainable use of water resources, etc., — issues of global concern.

The nature and dimension of challenges facing the national agricultural research systems are indeed varied, complex and daunting. The system's ability to come to grips with these will largely depend on its ability to tap resources and opportunities, but most importantly in chartering a shared vision of 'change' and putting in place mechanisms to steer the system-wide change through stepwise elaboration of the road map which integrates the varied perspectives and concerns of emerging challenges.

Elements of change which will be critical in transforming our operations include understanding and building a systems-thinking and perspective at all levels: What constitutes the system? In what way is the system framework growing, laterally or vertically? Do we need to redefine the roles of the system components and what kind of linkages/ complementarities need to be established and how? How does the system increasingly adopt systems-based approaches in conceiving, planning and implementing research for development agenda, moving from individual crop to farming system to landscape and ecological approaches. An important element of change will be to put in place mechanisms for research prioritisation at local, regional and national levels. Balancing research efforts towards solving problems of immediate nature and those requiring a longer-term perspective will be essential. Yet another important element of change will be to adopt region-specific approaches which take into account both sustainable use of natural resource endowments and the prevalent socio-economic features in defining and prioritising research agenda.

Adopting integrated approaches, the key to solving increasingly complex systembased problems will call for working in partnership amongst a range of stakeholders. Evolving mechanisms to permit and facilitate new ways of working will constitute an important element of the change agenda. Thus far a major demand on the research system has focused on technology generation for increased crop productivity. While this will continue to be important, the system additionally will be increasingly called upon to address policy research to guide the development direction and in turn be influenced by the emerging development paradigm.

India's agricultural research and education system is the primary organ which coordinates and contributes to enlarging the knowledge base required to improve the efficiency and productivity of the agriculture sector whose growth will continue to be a significant factor for improving livelihoods of the vast majority of the poor and the country's overall growth, development and economy. The system's ability to effectively capitalise on its vast physical network for creating, disseminating and utilising knowledge is what will enable us to be competitive in the emerging global scene. What we need is to put in place mechanisms which enable building a shared vision amongst key stakeholders, of ways in which the system must transform itself to cope with a multitude of challenges that we face. This will call for bringing on-board the best of expertise from a range of perspectives to collectively bear upon our understanding and to steer the change. System transformation will come about only through a step-wise progress, constantly analysing and seeking the best way forward.

References

Ashokkumar, Goba and Bhushan, Bharat, Funding of Open and Distance Higher Education in India. Quality & Policy Issues. *Uni. News*, Vol. 42(8), 14-24. 2004.

Bansil, P.C., *Economic Problems of Indian Agriculture*, CBS Pub, 2002.

John, Daniel, Open and Distance Learning Unlocking the Potential, *New Frontier in Education Int. J. Edue.* XXXII, 125-126.2002.

Lockwood F. and Goodey a. *Innovation in Open and Distance Learning*. Kogan page, London. 2001.

Madhukar, Indira, *Internet Based Distance Learning*. New Delhi, Authorpress. 2002.

Pattanaik, Bikram K., *Extension Education and Agriculture Development : An Assessment of Human Capacity Buildin*. The Associated Pub, 2006.

Thakur, Ghanshyam, *Challenges and Problems of Reforming Higher Education in India*, Sanjay Prakashan, 2004.

YCMOU, 2003. *Principles and Practices in Distance Education*. Yashwantrao Chavan Maharashtra Open University. Pub. 1177. 15 & 20.

6
Conclusion

Agricultural education in India dates back to early twentieth century with the establishment of agricultural schools in the country by the British rulers. Under the Indian context, agricultural education is generally considered as a pre-service training as a majority of the students are employed in the state governments in the department of agriculture. The primary aim of establishing agricultural colleges is to train and educate the students, so that they can engage in agricultural, carryout various activities in a scientific manner and thereby boost production. Similarly, these graduates are expected to be well equipped with knowledge scale required for employment in agriculture, public and private sector. In this modern age, it is imperative to know the choice of career of agricultural students and to prepare them for a satisfied living in their life, as agricultural education offers many job opportunities to plan and choose their career, to avoid frustration in their life.

Aspiration is considered as one of the important variables of personality of an individual. In this context, the present investigation has to be conceived as a contribution towards understanding of the nature and extent of aspiration of the students. Students have different socio-economic, psychological and cultural background. Also they differ in their earlier educational setting like, medium of instruction, system of education, peer circle, etc., with such varying backgrounds one cannot expect all the students to have similar aspirations. It is essential to understand the various aspirations and variations in aspirations existing among the boy and girl students of agricultural colleges because it decides their future career and hence the study has been attempted with the prime objective to find out the occupational aspiration differences existing among the undergraduate students of agricultural colleges.

A careful assessment of the occupational aspirations of these students will help the administrators and policy makers in fine tuning the curriculum to suit the requirement of the students. Therefore, the present study was conducted with the following objectives:

1. To study the personal and socio-economic profile of students.
2. To analyse the occupational aspiration level of students of different campuses.
3. To find out the occupational aspiration differences existing among the students of different college.
4. To find out the association between personal and socio-economic characteristics and occupational aspirations of students.
5. To study the sources of information utilised by students for occupation and job opportunities.

The study was conducted during September-December 2009 at the University of Agricultural Science, Bangalore in Karnataka state of India covering three campuses relating to Agriculture discipline viz., Agricultural College, GKVK, Bangalore, Agricultural college, Mandya and Agricultural college, Shimoga. The population consists of all the final year students of B.Sc (Agri.) from all the three campuses of the university. The data were collected from a purposively selected 120 students (40 from each college) with the help of well structured, pre-tested interview schedule, through the personal interview method.

The collected data were analysed using appropriate statistical tools and the dependent variable is occupational aspiration of students. The independent variables were age, sex, annual income, birthplace and native place, place of education, education level of mother, education level of father, father's occupation, mother's occupation, family type, sibling status and academic performance. The salient findings of the study are summarised hereunder:

Major Findings of the Study

The major findings of the study are as follows:

Personal and Socio-economic Profile of Students

1. A majority of the students in general belong to less than 21 years age group (57.50 per cent) followed by 22 to 23 years (35.00 per cent) and above 23 years group (7.50 per cent). A similar trend is observed with respect to students of different agricultural colleges wherein more than half of the students belong to below 21 years age group at GKVK (60.00 per cent), Mandya (60.00 per cent) and Shimoga (52.50 per cent) campuses
2. A great majority of the students were boys (84.20 per cent) followed by girls (15.80 per cent). Similar findings were true with respect to different colleges. Male domination was observed in GKVK (95.00 per cent), Mandya (82.50 per cent) and Shimoga campuses (75.00 per cent). Less than quarter of the students were girls in the above colleges.
3. A thumping majority of the students in total belong to rural areas both with respect to birth (76.70 per cent) as well as being native (95.80 per cent). Among students of different campuses, Shimoga campus had more rural students (85.00 per cent) followed by Mandya (62.50 per cent) and GKVK (82.50 per cent) with respect to birthplace. Similar observations were true with respect to native place.
4. A large majority of the students had primary education from rural areas (70.00 per cent) followed by urban areas (30.00 per cent). Regarding other types of education a reverse trend was observed with 93.3 per cent of students having secondary, 96.70 per cent high school and 96.70 per cent PUC education in urban areas.
5. Nearly three-fourths (70.00 per cent) of the fathers of students had secondary and above education followed by an equal number with primary education and illiterates (15.00 per cent). On further observation it shows that more than half of fathers of students in Shimoga campus (80.00 per cent), Mandya campus (62.50 per cent) and GKVK campus (67.50 per cent) belong to secondary and above education group.

6. Most of mothers of students in general (60.80 per cent) had secondary and above level of education followed by the illiterates (23.30 per cent) and the primary education group (15.00 per cent). A comparison among students of different campuses with respect to the mother's education shows that more number of Shimoga campus students, mothers belong to the secondary and above level of education followed by Mandya (55 per cent) and GKVK campus (52.50 per cent). More number of illiterates were found in GKVK (30.00 per cent) and Mandya campus (17.50 per cent) than Shimoga campus (12.50 per cent).
7. A majority of the fathers of students in general (60.80 per cent) had farming occupation followed by business (15.00 per cent). Among different campuses 70.00 per cent of GKVK College 60 per cent of fathers of Mandya College and 50 per cent of Father's of Shimoga College had farming occupation.
8. More than half of the mothers of students studying in different colleges (57.50 per cent) had farming occupation followed by government service (18.30 per cent) and business (10.90 per cent). A similar trend was observed with respect to mothers of students of different colleges viz., GKVK (75.00 per cent) Mandya (42.50 per cent) and Shimoga (55.00 per cent) having farming occupation.
9. In general nearly two-thirds (59.20 per cent) of the parents had an annual income of Rs.11,000 as against 40.80 per cent with an income of Rs. 11,000 and above. Among different campuses a similar trend was observed with 57.50 per cent of Shimoga, 52.50 per cent of Mandya and 67.50 per cent of GKVK parents belonging to the annual income category of Rs.11000 and below.
10. An overwhelming majority of the respondents in total belong to the nuclear family (70.00 per cent) and the remaining belong to the Joint family (30.00 per cent). A similar trend is seen with respect to students of different colleges, namely, GKVK (72.50 per cent), Mandya (65.00 per cent) and Shimoga (72.50 per cent) who belong to the nuclear family. On the other hand, 27.50 per cent in GKVK, 35.00 per cent in Mandya and 27.50 per cent in Shimoga belong to the joint family.

11. More than half of the respondents belong to 2-3 group (61.70 per cent) followed by 0-1 (27.50 per cent) and more than the group (10.80 per cent). More or less the same trend is seen with respect to students studying at GKVK (67.50 per cent), Mandya (60.00 per cent) and Shimoga campus (57.50 per cent) who belong to the 2-3 sibling status groups. Around one-third of students of different colleges viz. GKVK (25.00 per cent), Mandya (22.50 per cent) and Shimoga colleges (35.00 per cent) belong to the 0-1 category of sibling status.
12. More than half of the students (52.50 per cent) had obtained 7.0-8.5 grade points followed by less than 7.0 by 38.30 per cent and more than 8.5 by 9.2 per cent of students. Among different colleges, Shimoga campus students (67.50 per cent) were more in 7 to 8.5 GPA categories followed by GKVK (62.50 per cent) and Mandya (52.50 per cent) campus.

Occupational Aspiration Level of Students

13. Nearly two-thirds of the students in general (55.83 per cent) had a lower level of occupational aspiration and one-third of the students (34.17 per cent) had a higher level of aspiration. A similar trend of results was true with respect to students of different colleges. More than two- thirds of students of Agriculture College, GKVK belong to the low aspiration category (67.50 per cent) followed by students of Shimoga (52.50 per cent) and Mandya (47.50 per cent). In the high level of occupational aspiration group more number of Mandya students (40.00 per cent) followed by Shimoga (37.50 per cent) and GKVK students (25.00 per cent) were found.
14. No significant difference was observed with respect to the occupational aspiration level of students of different colleges as revealed by the results of ANOVA test.
15. A great majority of the students of Agricultural College, GKVK, preferred an administrative position in the department of agriculture followed by starting one's own business and getting an administrative job in government departments. The fourth rank went in favour of getting a

job in the cooperative sector followed by getting a job in panchayatiraj institutions, voluntary organisations and private companies. The least preferred occupation was to secure a job in central government.

16. In Agricultural College, Mandya, a majority of the students preferred an administrative position in the department of agriculture followed by getting administrative job in government departments and an academic position in agricultural university. The fourth rank went in favour of getting a job in private companies, followed by the corporate sector and panchayatiraj institutions. The least preferred occupation was to become a business analyst.
17. With respect to Agricultural College, Shimoga, a majority of the students preferred an academic position in agriculture university followed by getting an administrative job in government department and a job in a private company. The fourth rank went in fevour of starting one's own business, followed by an administrative position in the department of agriculture an nationalised bank and business occupation.
18. A majority of the students in general, preferred administrative job followed by academic position in agricultural university and a job in a private company. To start one's own business, to get a job in voluntary organisations and sales and business occupation were in the next order. The least preferred occupation was to become a business analyst.

Occupational Aspiration Preferences of Students

19. The students of Agricultural College, GKVK, preferred to enter into politics (22.50 per cent) as their third choice followed by securing administrative position in the department of agriculture (17.50 per cent) and securing job in voluntary organisations (15.00 per cent) as the least preferred occupations. The second preferred areas were to secure an administrative position in the department of agriculture (27.50 per cent) followed by securing job in cooperative sector (22.50 per cent) and undertake farming occupation. The first choices were in the order of securing

an administrative job (42.50 per cent), securing a central govt. job (27.50 per cent) and starting one's own consultancy in agriculture (20.00 per cent).

20. With respect to occupational aspiration preference of students of agricultural College, Mandya, the third preferred aspirations were to start sales and business occupation (20.00 per cent), undertake one's own farming occupation (20.00 per cent) and to enter politics (20.00 per cent). The second order preferences were to secure an administrative position in the department of agriculture (47.50 per cent), followed by the securing job in the cooperative sector (27.50 per cent) and panchayati raj institutions (27.50 per cent). The first preferred areas were in the order of securing administrative job (57.50 per cent) followed by becoming an agricultural university scientist (42.50 per cent) and to secure a job in central government (42.50 per cent).

21. The occupational aspirations as indicated by the students of Agricultural College, Shimoga, revealed that a majority of the students preferred to start their own business (30.00 per cent) followed by securing academic position in agricultural university (27.55 per cent) as their third preferred occupation. The second order occupations preferred were to secure an administrative position in the department of agriculture (32.50 per cent) followed by a securing a job in private company and nationalised bank (27.50 per cent) each. The first preferred occupations were in the order of securing an administrative job in government departments (60.00 per cent) followed by securing an academic position in agricultural university (47.50 per cent) and securing an administrative position in department of agriculture (42.50 per cent).

22. Regarding the occupational aspirations of students of different colleges at GKVK, Mandya and Shimoga, it is observed that most of the students liked to enter politics (23.30 per cent) followed by sales and business occupation (19.20 per cent) as their preferred occupations. The second preferred occupations were to secure an administrative position in the department of agriculture (32.50 per cent)

followed by securing a job in cooperative sector (25.80 per cent) and in nationalised banks (22.50 per cent). The students liked to secure an administrative job in government departments (53.30 per cent) followed by securing an administrative position in the department of agriculture (33.30 per cent) and securing an academic position in agricultural university (31.70 per cent) as their third preferred occupation.

Association between Personal and Socio-economic Characteristics and Aspiration level of Students.

23. A significant association was observed at 5 per cent level of significance between the level of education of father and mother and the annual income level of respondents and their occupational aspiration level at Agricultural College, GKVK
24. There existed a significant association among the education level of father, the education level of mother, father's occupation, birthplace and native place and occupational aspiration level of students of Agricultural College, Mandya as evidenced by the significant results of the chi-square test at 5 per cent level of significance.
25. A significant association between the education level of mother of students and father's occupation, and their occupational aspiration level was observed among the students of Agricultural College, Shimoga.
26. There is a significant association between the education level of father and mother, father's occupation, mother's occupation, academic performance and occupational aspiration level of students in general as revealed by the results of chi-square test. The other variables, namely, age, sex, annual income, birthplace and native place, family type, sibling status and place of education had no significant association with the occupational aspiration level of students.

Source of Information Utilised for Occupation and Job Placements.

27. A majority of the students in general used mass media sources to a maximum extent followed by informal and

formal sources. Among the mass media sources, most of the students used websites (67.5 per cent) followed by newspapers (62.50 per cent), television (35.00 per cent) and journals (20.00 per cent). Friends (66.66 per cent), parents (31.66 per cent) and relatives (27.50 per cent) among informal sources and university placement cell (30.83 per cent) agricultural officers (26.66 per cent) and consultants (19.16 per cent) among formal sources were utilised by a majority of the students in general.

28. With respect to Agricultural College, GKVK, websites (72.50 per cent) and journals (17.50 per cent) among mass media sources, friends (55.00 per cent), parents (22.50 per cent) and relatives among informal sources and university placement cell (27.50 per cent), consultants (17.50 per cent) and agricultural officers (15.00 per cent) among formal sources were consulted by most of the students for job placement.
29. Regarding Agricultural College, Mandya, the most utilised sources by the students were websites (62.50 per cent), newspapers (62.50 per cent) and television (52.50 per cent) among mass media sources, friends (75.00 per cent), relatives (45.00 per cent), and neighbors (32.50 per cent) among informal sources and university placement cell (45.00 per cent), consultants (32.50 per cent) and agricultural officers (35.00 per cent) among formal sources.
30. A large majority of the students of Agricultural College, Shimoga consulted websites (70.00 per cent), newspapers (67.50 per cent), and television (27.50 per cent), among mass media sources. Friends (70.00 per cent), parents (40.00 per cent), and neighbours (27.50 per cent), among informal sources and agricultural officers (30.00 per cent), and University placement cell (20.00 per cent), among formal sources were consulted by a good number of students for job placement information.

Implications of the Study

An introspective analysis of the findings of the study implied the following:

1. An interesting finding of the study is that a majority of the students wanted to secure an administrative position in the government department in general and the department of agriculture in particular. The teacher counsellors and parents should try to understand their specific aspirations, and guide and support them technically, financially as well as morally. The university may start a consultancy centre for agricultural students in order to guide them in fulfilling their aspirations.
2. A considerable number of students had aspired for working in voluntary organisations. It is therefore recommended that the groups of like-minded agricultural graduates may be encouraged to establish voluntary organisations in their areas which will give an impetus to the agricultural and rural development activities.
3. The study pointed out that farming has been the third preferred occupation next only to the administrative position in development departments and agricultural universities. It indicates that they are not willing to take risk by setting up an agri-entrepreneurship. Hence, it is recommended that capacity building of farm graduates through hands-on-training should be strengthened, besides promoting appropriate enterprise combinations using appropriate extension strategies and financial market-led extension approaches. The financial institutions also take efforts for provision of subsidies to agri-entrepreneurship, which would increase income and generate employment in rural areas.
4. The findings should be taken into consideration by the planners and policy makers while designing the plans and policies for higher education and placement of farm graduates. The suggestions made by the students for fulfilling their aspirations may also be considered as guidelines for designing such plans and policies.
5. It is suggested to motivate students for entering farming by providing incentives to them for developing infrastructure facilities in farming.
6. The variables like parent's education, parent's occupation and academic preference had significant association with

occupational aspiration levels of students. These characteristics have to be kept in mind while tailoring programmes to satisfy the needs of students by educational institutions.

7. As mass media sources were consulted more by a large majority of the respondents, efforts need to be made to increase the mass media exposure which will help in selecting preferred jobs by students.
8. The university has to design special programmes to help the students to get involved inuniversity life. Such programmes include academic and counselling orientation programmes for students, personal and career skill seminars, work opportunities, extracurricular activities, and integrated residence based programmes. Equipped with information on composition of its students, universities can determine the services that will best meet the particular needs of their students.

Suggestions for Future Research

1. Very few researches have been done to know the congruency between aspirations and attainment. More research should be done to explore the nature and extent of relationship between aspirations and attainment. This will really help to determine whether the aspirations are the determinant of occupational attainment.
2. A comparative analysis of occupational aspirations of students of different degree programmes.
3. Comparison of aspirations of undergraduate and postgraduate students, and boys and girls.

Bibliography

Abijith, T.K., 2002, Impact Analysis of Rural Agricultural Work Experience Programe, M.Sc (Ag.) Thesis, (Unpublished), TNAU, Coimbatore.

Arunachalam, R., and S.Somasundaram. 2000, A Study on Aspiration differences existing among the undergraduate girls students of different campuses in Tamil Nadu Agricultural University. *Journal of Educational research and Extension*.37: 11-19.

Ashok Kumar, B.R., 2004, A study on the Achievement Motivation and Usefulness of Agriculture Curriculum asperceved by Students at University of Agricultural Sciences, Bangalore. M.Sc. (Agric.) thesis, (Unpub.) University of Agricultural Sciences, Bangalore.

Babitha, J. and Somasundaram, D., 2003, Aspirations of Under-Graduate Girl Students in Different Campuses of Tamil Nadu Agricultural University. *Journal of Extension Education,* 14 (1&2): 3501-3502.

Behra, P., 1986, A study of Socio-Economic Status, Locus of Control and Personality Adjustment of High School Students. *Journal of Educational Research and Extension,* 23(1): 9-15

Bhatnagar, J.K., and M. Sharma, 1992, A study of relationship between Parental Education and academic Achievement in a seminar setting. *Psychological Studies,* Calicut, 37(2&3):126-129.

Burchinal, C. L., 1970, Differences in educational and occupational aspirations of farm, small town and city boys. *Rural Sociology,* 26 (2): 107-118.

Chauhan, K. N. K., Sinha, B. P. and Mehta, P., 1978, Impact of farm telecasts on farmers level of aspirations. *Society and Culture,* 9: 23-36.

Dempo, 1944, Level aspirations. In J. McV Munt (Ed.) Personality and the *Behaviour Disorders,* 6: 146-149.

Halakatti, Sunil, V. and Ravi, M. S., 1987, Job and subject preference for post graduate studies among agricultural graduates. *Indian Psychological Review,* 48 (2): 79-83.

Haller, A. O. and Sewell, W. H., 1957, Farm Residence and level of education and occupational aspirations. *American Journal of Sociology,* 62: 407-411.

1966, Occupational choices of rural youth. *Journal of Cooperative Extension,* 4 (1): 93- 101

Hoover, K.N., 1963, *Handbook of Agricultural Occupations,* The Interstate Printers and Publishers, Inc., Illinois.

Hosur, G.P., 1977, A Study on Achievement Motivation of Gramasevaks of Dharwad District, Karnataka. M.Sc. (Ag.) thesis (unpub) University of Agricultural Sciences, Bangalore.

Kuvlesky, W. P. and Bealer. R., 1967, The relevance or adolescent occupational aspirations for subsequent job attainments. *Rural Sociology,* 32 (3): 290-301.

Lewin, 1951, *Level of aspirations—In personality and behaviour disorders* (Ed.) I-runt, Donald Press, New York.

Madhu Asthana and Srivastava, B.K., 1992, Level of aspirations in Science and arts students. *Indian Psychological Review,* 38 (4-5): 27-29.

Makhiji, V.R. and Singh, S.P., 1987, Evaluating Training Adequacy for Effective Management of Under-Graduate Agriculture Programme. *Indian Journal of Extension Education,* 23 (1&2): 7-12.

Manisha, V.I. and Sawant, P.A., 2001, Educational and Aspirations of Girl Students. *Maharshtra Journal of Extension Education,* 20: 22-24.

Marini, M.M.and Greenberger. 1997, Sex differences in occupational aspirations and expectations, *AUCC Research file* 1 (5): 1-12.

Mathur, S.K. and T.V. Rao 1975. Patterns of Aspirations and Apprehension of student's of different Professional College. *Journal of Educational Research and Extension.*12 (1): 31-37.15.

Meenaben, C., Patel, and N.B. Chauhan. 2005. Pattern of Internet Use by Agricultural students. *Agricultural Extension Review.*15: 13-15.

Muthayya, B. C., 1971, *Farmers and their aspirations, influence of socio-economic status and work orientation.* National Institute of Community Development, Hyderabad.

Narendran, K., 2000, Occupational Aspirations of rural youth in Kolar district of Karnataka state. M.Sc. (Ag.) thesis (Unpublished), University of Agricultural Science Bangalore.

Negga, E.M., 1987, Factors Influencing Academic Achievement of Under-Graduate Students of Agriculture. M.Sc. (Ag.) Thesis, Unpublished. TNAU, Coimbatore.

Opplot, J.A., 1984, Occupational Aspirations of Primary School Leavers in Uganda. *Uganda Journal,* 41: 1-7.

Pandey, R., 1974, Rural-urban comparison of occupational aspirations of college youth. *The Indian Journal of Social Work*. 23 (2): 121-136.

Pareek, U. and Trivedi, G., 1964, Categorisation of Rural Socio- economic groups.The *Indian Journal of Social Work,* 24: 287-303.

Pradhan, G.C., 2001, Factors Affecting Occupational Aspiration of College youths. *University News Journal,* 39 (50): 10-14.

2002, Factors affecting Occupational Aspiration of College youths. *Journal of Educational Research and Extension*.39: 38-47.

Preston, 1944, Level of aspirations. In J. MeV Munt (Ed.) P*ersonality and the Behaviour Disorders,* 6: 146-149.

Rajasekaran, R., 1999, Impact of RAWE Programme in Experimental Learning.Unpub. Ph.D. Topical Research Report, TNAU, Coimbatore.

Rao, K. N., 1964, A study of Needs, Interests, Aspirations and leisure time activities of school going boys in Kanjhawala block. *M.sc. (Agril),* thesis (Unpublished), I.A.R.I New Delhi.

Rexlin, R., 1993, Perception of Horticultural Students Towards Self Employment. Unpub. Topical Research Report, TNAU, Madurai.

Robert, J.M., 1985, Prediction of Academic Success and Persistence as Functions of Patterns and Background Information. Dissertation Abstract International: *The Humanities and Social Science,* University Microfilms, Michigan, 42(2): 429-431.

Russel, M. and Charles, G. M., 1959, Community of Orientation and Occupational aspirations of Ninth grade students. *American Journal of Sociology,* 38: 303-308.

Sagane, M., 1979, A study of rural youth involvement in high yielding variety programme. M.Sc. (Agri) thesis (Unpublished), Punjab Rao Krishi Vidya Peet, Ludihana.

Sajeev, M.V., 2003, An Analysis of RAWEP of two Southern Agricultural Universities, M.Sc. Thesis (unpublished), UAS, Bangalore.

Sajid, A.K. and Nusrat, A.K., 1990, A study of level of aspirations and frustration in relation to Socio economic status of Twelfth grade students. *Indian Psychological Review,* 35 (3-4): 1-4.

Samuel, B.O., 1993, Academic Achievement and extra-Curricular Participation of Agricultural Under-Graduate Students of TNAU. M.Sc. (Ag.) *Thesis,* (Unpublished).TNAU, Madurai.

Sharma, R.P. and M.P. Dantare., 1995, A Study on Occupational Aspirations of School Going Youth of Madhya Pradesh. *Journal of Educational Research and Extension*.31: 130-133.

Sharma, R. R., 1987, A study of educational aspirations in relation to socio-economic status. *Journal of Institute of Educational Research,* 10 (4): 7-9.

Subramanyam, V.S., 1975, Professional Choices among Graduate Students in Agriculture. *Madras Agricultural Journal,* 62(10-12): 759.

Sundaraswami, B., Manjunath, L., J.G. Angadi and V.S. Yadav, 1997, Attitude of B.Sc. (Ag.) Students towards Agriculture. *Journal of Extension Education,* 8(5): 1572-1576.

Suryawanshi, R.B., and V.T. Wattamwai. 2003, A Study of Aspirations of the post graduate students of college of agriculture, Parbhani. *Maharashtra Journal of Extension Education.* 22: 117-121.

Trivedi, G., 1963, Measurement and analysis of socio-economic status of rural families. Ph. D. Thesis (unpublished), IARI, New Delhi.

Waman, G.K., Girase, K.A., and Desai. 2000, Aspiration and Employment of Agricultural Graduates. *Maharashtra Journal of Extension Education,* 19: 141-144.

Warwadekar S.C. Nirban A.J and Kadam J.R. 2007: Career Aspirations and needs of the higher secondary school students. *Asian Journal of Education.*27 (1&2):46-51.

Index